IMAGES
of America

DICKENSON
COUNTY

IMAGES
of America

DICKENSON
COUNTY

Victoria L. Osborne

ARCADIA
PUBLISHING

Published by Arcadia Publishing
Charleston, South Carolina

Library of Congress Catalog Card Number: 2006935463

For all general information contact Arcadia Publishing at:
Telephone 843-853-2070
Fax 843-853-0044
E-mail sales@arcadiapublishing.com
For customer service and orders:
Toll-Free 1-888-313-2665

Visit us on the Internet at www.arcadiapublishing.com

CONTENTS

ACKNOWLEDGMENTS

Dennis Reedy of Clinchco, Virginia, is owed a great debt of thanks for his efforts to preserve the history of Southwest Virginia. Thanks go to Aaron Davies of the Ralph Stanley Museum and Norma Morris, publicist for Ralph Stanley. Ralph Stanley is thanked for his insight into Dickenson County. Thanks also go to the Dickenson County Library for its help in the history of the county, the Washington County Historical Society, and the Southwest Virginia Historical and Preservation Society for opening its archives. I also wish to thank my editor, Courtney Hutton, for her tireless assistance.

FOREWORD

When one thinks of Dickenson County they think of Virginia's baby county. I think of it as home. I've traveled throughout the United States, visiting all 50 states and 14 countries. But all pale in comparison to my home in Dickenson County. I always look forward to returning to my home, and it never disappoints me. For me growing up in Dickenson was a fun-filled time with my friends and brother, Carter. We would often attend the trials of the day and listen to the lawyers argue their cases and Judge Galley Friend make his rulings. Our lives were filled with family and neighbors, a life where respect of God and family governed our every action. The greatest influence in my life was my mother, who had a faith in our music and encouraged Carter and myself to pursue that gift to make it a reality. I modeled my style in the early days after Bill Monroe and the Carter Family. Later my own style emerged. We often played at the Morgan Theatre that is now the Jettie Baker Center, and I fondly remember those as the good old days. This year and this month of October 2006 makes my 60th year in the music business, and I have had the pleasure of seeing the musical legacy continue in my son and grandson. Dr. Osborne shows the reader in this Images of America series that the way of life in Dickenson County was hard but filled with love and respect of God and family, with an appreciation of the gifts that God gave us.

—Dr. Ralph Stanley

INTRODUCTION

Dickenson County was formed in 1880 from parts of Wise, Russell, and Buchanan Counties. The county was named for William J. Dickenson, a state legislator from Russell County who was the patron for the bill in the house of delegates in 1880 to establish Dickenson as the 100th county in Virginia. Dickenson would be forever known as Virginia's baby county.

Some of the senate members wanted to name the county "Stonewall" in honor of Gen. Stonewall Jackson. The bill was approved by Gov. Frederick W. M. Holliday. The county seat was first located near the mouth of Caney Fork on the McClure River. It was named Ervinton in honor of Micajah Ervin, one of the early settlers. The first circuit court was held on May 30, 1881, with Judge John A. Kelly presiding. The courthouse was rebuilt in 1884 and remodeled in 1915–1916, and it contained fireproof vaults for the clerk and treasurer.

Daniel Boone may have been one of the earliest white settlers. In the autumn of 1767, he and two others traveled northward from their homes on the Yadkin River in North Carolina and reached the headwaters of the West (later called Russell) Fork of the Big Sandy River. The first hunters found Dickenson a paradise. Hunters would make camp, hunt, and prepare skins for many months before returning to their homes; thus they became known as the Long Hunters. Richard "Fighting Dick" Colley made the first white settlement three miles south of Haysi. Legend has it he killed a black bear with his own hands. In the mid-1700s, John Swift met a man by the name of George Mundy. Mundy had been held captive by Native Americans in the Great Wilderness for about three years before he escaped. Mundy had an extensive knowledge of silver mines, which Swift found interesting. At the mouth of Roaring Fork on the McClure River and south of the mountains, prospectors dug for silver. The mine was located in a large laurel thicket. Three mines were opened, and Swift's company built a furnace for smelting ore. The first venture ended in 1760 a great success. At that point, the groups divided into two teams. One went to Kentucky and the other went southwest. No more silver was ever found. Legend says that silver is still in the Cumberland Mountains.

The only known Revolutionary War soldier buried in Dickenson County rests on a knoll east of McClure and Mullins.

The county's economy has always been dependent upon natural resources—first, game and fur; second, timber; and third; coal. Wash Brittin (or Briton), of Brittin and Pennsylvania Company, began the timber industry around 1867. The first contract for sale of timber was made by A. D. Alley to Horsley and Tate in 1885. The W. M. Ritter Lumber Company bought most of the valuable timber in the county and was a major employer. The first contract recorded for minerals in Dickenson County occurred in 1886 when Richard Hibbitts sold a tract of coal land at 50¢ an acre to G. V. Litchfield. The Steinman Development Company was the first organization of its kind to buy coal deposits in Dickenson County. The Steinmans first purchased 1,000 acres on Cranes Nest River (then in Wise County) from Philip Fleming in December 1874. Times were hard, and every resource was used to supply the everyday needs. Men's everyday clothes were made from flax due to the strength of the material. Homes were built of hewn logs and roofs of boards and dirt or puncheon floors (hewn logs). The people were sociable on the occasions that they had to get together (workings, corn husking, fencings, log rolling, church, and weddings). Quilt gatherings were called workings and were often followed by a party where neighbors could continue to socialize. The day-to-day life was hard and strenuous.

Coal mining began on a large scale in 1916. Clinchfield Coal Corporation was the largest coal producer in Dickenson County. They built one of the county's major towns, Clinchco, around that same year. The Virginia Banner Coal Corporation built the town of Trammel. Splashdam Coal Corporation and Bartlich were built by Bartlich Coal Mining Company. In 1947, Clinchfield Coal opened the Moss No. 1 Preparation Plant and Moss No. 1 Mine. This operation was the largest coal mine in the world at the time. Averaging 200 railroad cars a day, they loaded their one-millionth car on August 11, 1982. In 1979, Clinchfield installed an even larger operation near the county on Caney Creek. This operation was called McClure No. 1 Mine and McClure River Preparation Plant. It was also the largest coal mine in the world for its time. In June 1932, the area suffered a mining tragedy at Splashdam Coal Corporation when an explosion killed 10 men. The probable cause of the explosion was an accumulation of methane gas (firedamp). When the gas, exploded coal dust in the mine was ignited.

The Carolina, Clinchfield, and Ohio Railway was completed in 1915. The last spike was driven at Trammel by the railroad's former president, George L. Carter. Fremont Station was named for John C. Fremont, a renowned western adventurer and explorer known as the "Pathfinder." He was the first Republican candidate to run for the office of president but was defeated by James Buchanan in the 1856 election. Supposedly Fremont was a surveyor on one of the small predecessor lines that eventually became part of Clinchfield. The station was used as a waiting room for passengers and a three-door freight room. By 1919, the freight business had grown so successful that it became necessary to lengthen the freight section by 50 feet, giving three additional doors to each side, and to construct 16 more feet of office space on the north end. The building has remained unchanged since 1919. Before the Fremont station opened, most goods coming into the area were hauled by horse- or mule-drawn wagons from Coeburn, a station on the Norfolk and Western Railway. The station served the businesses in Clintwood, the county stores of the surrounding areas, and the W. M. Ritter Lumber Company operations.

Dickenson County has retained its traditional culture of the Appalachian Mountains. The Breaks Interstate Park was created in 1954 by joint action of the Virginia and Kentucky Legislatures and encompasses 4,500 acres of natural beauty, including the largest canyon east of the Mississippi River at nearly five miles long and 1,600 feet deep.

The first recorded murder in the area occurred in 1817 near Abner's Gap. Sylvanius Brewer, Samuel Endicutt, and others were hunting, and Brewer and Endicutt had an argument over Brewer's wife. Brewer shot and killed Endicutt in the woods and left his body propped against a tree. When Endicutt was missed by others in the party, Brewer claimed not to know what happened. He even joined the search party that found Endicutt. He was arrested, tried, and convicted of the killing. Brewer was hung for the crime.

The first school in Dickenson County was established about 1855 at the mouth of Honey Branch about one and a half miles below Trammel. The first schools were subscription schools, where the teachers were paid a fixed monthly rate (usually $1 or $2) for each pupil. The first school bus was a homemade wooden shed mounted on a 1924 Chevrolet chassis. The bus had wooden seats and a small opening at the back of the door. This bus was owned by W. J. Artrip, who was paid $2.49 a day for its use. Bear Ridge School, in service from 1930 to 1970, was the last log school building to be used in the county.

On June 8, 1948, the town elections in Clintwood, Virginia, drew national and international attention when the voters elected an all-female town council and mayor. Minnie "Sis" Matter was elected mayor. The ladies took office in September 1948. Letters were received from around the world wishing them luck and expressing amazement that an all-woman government could be elected anywhere. The State Department featured the story in its *Voice of America* broadcast. By all accounts, the "Petticoat Government" was highly successful, and during their administration, many important improvement projects were undertaken, including expanding parking in town and installing parking meters in the downtown area. The area has produced a number of famous individuals.

The Bear Pen Dirty Socks baseball team was invited to Kansas to participate in the national semi-pro playoff series. Their record for that year was 23-2. Claude Fuller was nicknamed "Iron Man," a name that was given to him by R. L. Palmer, his boss at the No. 9 Mine in Clinchco. Fuller never missed a shift and would work two shifts a day. He could pitch left-handed and bat right-handed. The Iron Man signed with the New York Yankees for $168 a week and played minor-league ball for six weeks. Congressman John W. Flannagan Jr., "the Clintwood Cyclone," was one of the county's most prominent politicians, representing the "Fighting Ninth" congressional district. The John Flannagan Dam is named for him. The county is home to bluegrass legend Ralph Stanley.

One

BIRTH OF A BABY

DICKENSON COUNTY MARKER. Dickenson County is 335 square miles and includes the Breaks Interstate Park. The county's economy has long been dependent upon natural resources—first, game, second, timber, and third, coal. The first timber industry began around 1867 with a man named Wash Brittin and the Brittin and Pennsylvania Company. The first contract for sale of timber was made by A. D. Alley to Horsley and Tate in 1885. The first deed for poplar trees was made by Almarine Owens to Stephen Bitely in 1887. In 1909, the Yellow Poplar Lumber Company built a concrete splash dam for the purpose of moving logs through the Breaks area. At one time, this structure was the world's largest concrete splash dam. The structure currently supports a highway bridge. Now farming is on a small scale. (Photograph courtesy of the Southwest Virginia Historical and Preservation Society.)

DICKENSON-BUNDY COURTHOUSE. In 1786, Russell County was established. At that time, it represented the areas that are now Lee, Scott, Wise, Dickenson, Buchanan, and Tazewell Counties. This log house, part of which was used in the Dickenson-Bundy Log House, was built on the north side of the Clinch River in 1769 by Henry and Elizabeth Dickenson. (Photograph courtesy of the Southwest Virginia Historical and Preservation Society.)

OLD COURTHOUSE MARKER. The marker shows the site for the Old Russell County Courthouse. The highway marker program was started in Virginia in 1926 to designate historic sites, places, and battles. The original courthouse was built of logs by Henry Dickenson at Dickensonville. It burned during the Revolutionary War. This structure was used as a courthouse until 1818. (Photograph courtesy of the Southwest Virginia Historical and Preservation Society.)

HENRY DICKENSON'S LEGACY. Henry Dickenson had a distinguished beard that made him noticeable from distance. He built the original Dickenson-Bundy courthouse. The first court was held in the home of William Robinson at Castlewood on May 1, 1786. Justices included Alexander Barnett, Henry Smith, David Ward, Andrew Cowan, Samuel Richie, Thomas Carter, Henry Dickenson, and John Thompson. Later justices John Tate and Richard Price were added. The courthouse burned during the Revolutionary War. Henry Dickenson then constructed a two-story stone structure at a cost of $2,188.97. This structure was used as a courthouse until 1818 and is still referred to as the "Old Courthouse." When the senate proposed a 100th county, members wanted to name it "Stonewall" in honor of Gen. Stonewall Jackson. The county would have over 100 communities during its first 90 years in existence. (Photograph courtesy of the Southwest Virginia Historical and Preservation Society.)

DICKENSON COUNTY COURTHOUSE. The Dickenson County Courthouse in Clintwood was once referred to as the "wedding capital" of the area due to the large number of weddings that took place in the building. However, not all business conducted in the building is as pleasant; the area's most notorious criminals have found themselves there for trials and sentencing. (Photograph courtesy of the Southwest Virginia Historical and Preservation Society.)

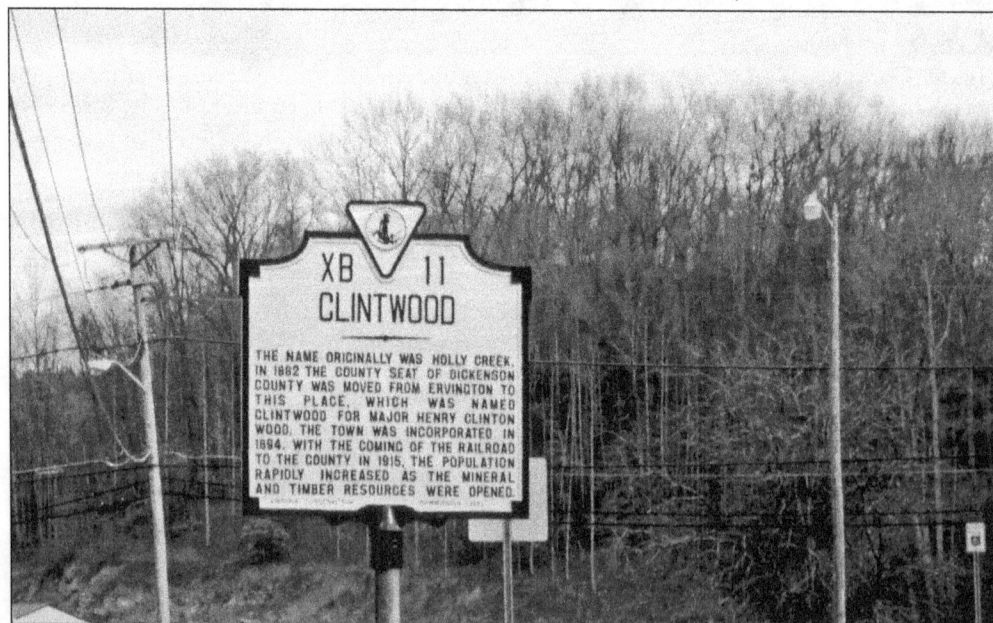

HISTORIC HOLLY CREEK. Clintwood is one of three cities incorporated in Dickenson County, the other two being Clinchco and Haysi. The original name for Clintwood was Holly Creek. In 1882, the county seat was moved from Ervinton to Clintwood. This historic marker was the result of the commonwealth's program to mark historic sites for travelers. (Photograph courtesy of the Southwest Virginia Historical and Preservation Society.)

THE KILLING ROCK OF 1892. The scene at the Killing Rock is depicted in Mrs. Joan Powers Meade's work. The tragedy took place at Pound Gap on May 14, 1892. On that date, Dr. M. B. "Doc" Taylor, Calve Fleming, and Calve's brother Herman Fleming allegedly came out of the woods and began to shoot, killing Ira Mullins, his wife, Wilson Mullins, and a boy, who were making their way across the mountain in a heavily loaded wagon. John Chappel, Greenberry Harris, Jane Mullins (Wilson's wife), and John Mullins escaped. (Photograph courtesy of Dennis Reedy.)

THE CHICKEN MYSTERY SOLVED. The W. M. Ritter Lumber Company Store at McClure served the community for many years. The "chicken roost mystery" revolved around the allegation of stolen chickens, which showed up under the store. They became dinner. The only telephone in the camp was located at the store. (Photograph courtesy of Dennis Reedy).

SCAFFOLD AT WORK. Mrs. Meade's painting shows the scaffold at work in the 1890s. The painting was done from an old photograph. After the murders at Killing Rock, Doc Taylor was apprehended, tried, and convicted. He was hung for his offenses. There are four methods of hanging: the long, short, and standard drops, as well as suspension hanging. The short-drop method was used in the United States until the 19th century, when the long drop was introduced. The short drop could be a prolonged affair and was primarily for the entertainment of the public. The last public hanging was Rainey Bethea in 1936. (Photograph courtesy of Dennis Reedy.)

LICK CREEK LOGGING CAMP. The Lick Creek camp around 1927 looked much like this photograph. All camps were kept neat and clean at all times. A lobby boy swept the floors, made and changed the beds, and built and tended fires in the kitchen and lobby. In addition to the camp cars on wheels, there were also a number of portable camp houses. (Photograph courtesy of Dennis Reedy.)

RITTER COMPANY STORES. In 1925, the Ritter stores offered nine kinds of coffee, women's rayon ready-to-wear, Victrolas and Kodaks, and merchant tailors that would come in to measure for a suit. Another hot item at the store was radios. One famous brand featured was the Atwater Kent radio, which was a relatively new brand. Arthur Atwater Kent had 93 patents at his death. (Photograph courtesy of Dennis Reedy.)

THE HOTEL MCCLURE. In the upper left of this photograph is the Hotel McClure around 1920. The two steam-heated sheds are where lumber that had been kiln-dried and planed was stored, especially flooring. By controlling the heat and humidity in the sheds, the lumber was kept from warping. Also visible are the planing mill, where lumber was surfaced, and the dry kiln, just beyond. (Photograph courtesy of Dennis Reedy.)

UNCLE SAM'S HOUSE. The house of "Uncle Sam" Ramsey was featured in the 1929 issue of *Hardwood Bark* magazine. The house was built entirely with Ritter lumber, with chestnut bark off the Ritter logs covering the exterior and giving it an attractive appearance. The porch ports are small tresses with the bark left on. (Photograph courtesy of Dennis Reedy.)

RAILROAD CREW AT WORK. This railroad crew works on the Calvin Fork of Lick Creek in 1933. From left to right are (first row) William Anderson (on horse), James Deel, Harvey Powers, Claude Johnson, Frank Wright, John Selfe, Albert Powers, and Sam Counts (foreman); (standing on push car) Noah Walker Counts and Arvil Counts. Sam Counts started work for Ritter as a railroad foreman in 1918. (Photograph courtesy of Dennis Reedy.)

RAIL CONSTRUCTION AT LICK CREEK. This railroad construction crew works on the Rush Branch of Lick Creek in 1923. From left to right are (seated and kneeling) Henry Duty, Alamander Silcox, ? Porter, and Sam Counts, the foreman; (standing) Carron Hay, Bill Cook, unidentified, Arvil Counts, Rual Counts, John Selfe, Holly Ray Edwards, Muncie Bostic, and Starlin Duty. The Ritter Company later moved to Frying Pan. (Photograph courtesy of Dennis Reedy.)

MCCLURE LUMBER PLANT. The McClure Lumber Plant received the "E" Award during World War II, the "E" standing for excellence. The award consisted of a large flag or pennant, which was flown over the mill after the presentation of lapel pins for a job well done to staff and employees. Lumber products manufactured at McClure during World War II were used in landing and assault boats, sub chasers, mine sweepers, tugs, and PT boats, as well as Coast Guard patrol boats. Wood materials were also used in truck bodies. It was with World War II that many women found themselves going to work in the factories while husbands, brothers, fathers, and boyfriends went to fight in the war. After the war ended, the women didn't just return to the kitchens and children. Thus the introduction of women into the workforce that had been reserved for men was a direct result of World War II. (Photograph courtesy of Dennis Reedy.)

ENGINE NO. 10. Engine No. 10, pictured before the conversion from standard to narrow gauge, works as shifter at McClure around 1925. Note the large oil light on the engine. It is carrying a carload of 1-by-2¾-by-19-inch oak heading for the dry kiln, later to be worked into parquet flooring, W. M. Ritter's most famous product. The Appalachian oak flooring was manufactured at the planing mill. The small pieces of flooring known as parquet came in sizes from 9 inches to 18 inches. Parquet was laid in three distinct patterns: block, basket weave, and herringbone. Some of the smaller pieces could be glued together or fastened together with metal strips to form blocks. They were sanded, varnished, passed under lights to dry, and polished. (Photograph courtesy of Dennis Reedy.)

BEAVER CREEK RAILROAD. Foreman E. B. Dehart and his railroad crew are hard at work building a new railroad at Beaver Camp. W. M. Steele is handling the crane. Supplies such as coal, oil, and parts were hauled to the shovel on a horse-drawn sled. The logging railroad is sometimes referred to as a tram road. It was an essential part of Ritter operations. (Photograph courtesy of Dennis Reedy.)

ENGINE NO. 4. The No. 4 C/N 929 and its crew poses with a load of logs at Bear Pen Gap in 1924. Ritter owned 45 Shays. Eleven were used in Dickenson County and were maintained at the McClure Shop, which was under the supervision of "Uncle Sam" Ramsey. A fleet of 64 log cars as well as several boxcars was serviced there. (Photograph courtesy of Dennis Reedy.)

FRYING PAN TIES. Tom Ratliff, the crew boss in front, poses with his crew. From left to right are unidentified, Starlin Duty, Bill Deel, Montague Bostic, unidentified, Bryan Edwards, Henry Duty, and Basil Bostic. The railroad crew is hauling a load of oak ties near Frying Pan. The companies liked to photograph the area and its employees. (Photograph courtesy of Dennis Reedy.)

RITTER LUMBER WORKS. Ritter Lumber Company trucks loaded with large boards were a common sight. The capacity of the double mill at McClure was 80,000 feet a day. The two sections of the mill were seldom used at once, especially during the Great Depression beginning in 1929. The McClure mill averaged 42,419 feet a day for the first six months of 1928. (Photograph courtesy of Dennis Reedy.)

CLINCHCO IS BORN. These stately buildings line Main Street in Clinchco in 1920. Clinchco was built by the Clinchfield Coal Corporation in 1923. Clinchco is near the Carolina, Clinchfield, and Ohio (CC&O) Railroad and served as a mining camp. Around 1917, the Clinchfield Coal Company began mining at Clinchco, where land was bought for 10¢ to 15¢ an acre. (Photograph courtesy of Dennis Reedy.)

GULF IS BORN. As Dickenson County developed, new businesses emerged. Next to John Tipton's house, Turner Auto Sales, Inc., and the Riverside Motor Company were two of the new businesses in Riverside. Notice Turner Auto Sales endorsed and sold Gulf products. It was common for a company to identify with only one major brand in an attempt to gain consumer loyalty to them alone. (Photograph courtesy of Dennis Reedy.)

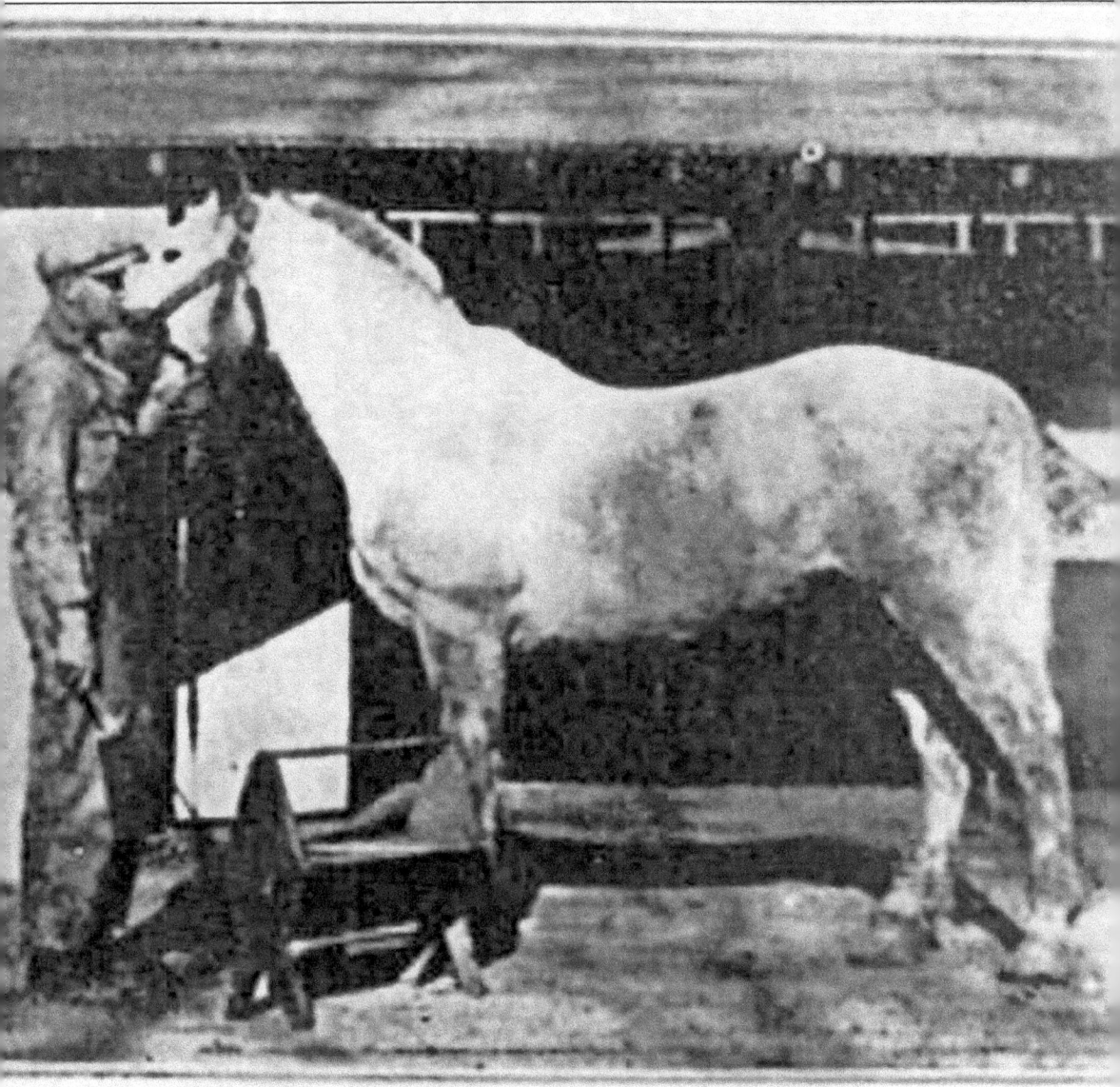

HUSKIES AT WORK. Blacksmith Frank Fletcher is pictured alongside Dutch at Lick Creek Camp around 1928. The work required of the huskies (heavy horses bred for farming and other heavy work) was often dangerous. Sometimes the logs would skid too fast, and the horses were able to dart into a clearing, releasing them from the logs, when the team driver called out "Jay-hole!" That meant the logs could continue to proceed down the hill while the horse was away from the danger. Companies regarded the animals as more valuable than the employees. The blacksmith who shod horses was a farrier. A blacksmith could usually double as a blade smith and locksmith. He could do repairs to logging chains and axe heads. (Photograph courtesy of Dennis Reedy.)

SECRET TO SUCCESS. Grady Baker is pictured with his sidekick, Peanut. Baker had an interesting philosophy about success; he was often quoted by friends as saying, "In order to be a success in life, never make the same mistake twice"—quite an interesting statement for a hardworking man that took a simplistic approach to the age-old question. (Photograph courtesy of Dennis Reedy.)

DICK AND CLYDE. Teamster Ralph Keller poses with Dick (left) and Clyde in 1921. The horses were said to be the best that money could buy. The men who drove the teams were known as team drivers or teamsters. A team could pull several logs at a time depending on the size of the logs and the terrain. (Photograph courtesy of Dennis Reedy.)

W. M. RITTER. W. M. Ritter, the founder and president of the W. M. Ritter Lumber Company, is seen here around 1940. Ritter, the youngest of 10 children, was the son of Franklin and Elizabeth Morris Ritter, who was a member of the Morris family that produced Robert Morris of Philadelphia, the Revolutionary patriot who largely financed the colonies in their struggle against the mother country. (Photograph courtesy of Dennis Reedy.)

RITTER'S FIRST OFFICE. This was the W. M. Ritter Lumber Company's first office at Welsh, West Virginia, used from 1896 until 1899. In 1899, the offices were moved to Columbus, Ohio. In 1903, the general office was moved from the Schultz Building to the Harrison Building, later called the Huntington Bank Building. In 1915, the general office was moved to the Peruna Building. (Photograph courtesy of Dennis Reedy.)

DOUBLE BAND MILL. The W. M. Ritter Lumber Company's mill at McClure in the 1920s had a daily capacity of 80,000 board feet. The building with the three tall stacks was the boiler room. In front of the boiler room was the water tank for the Shay engines. The physical plant and accompanying structures at McClure were similar to those at Fremont but on a larger scale. A planing mill and dry kiln serving both operations were built at McClure during 1918–1919. (Photograph courtesy of Dennis Reedy.)

WORKER SALARY BASE. The men were paid different wages from 10¢ to 15¢ an hour according to the jobs they performed. The men had to pay 60¢ a day for food and lodging at the boardinghouse. If they rented company housing, the rent was deducted from their paychecks. There were other deductions such as electric and medical bills. Advances on paychecks would also be deducted. If they bought items in advance at the company store, those deductions would also be withheld. Many times, the workers received no pay or owed money on payday. (Photograph courtesy of Dennis Reedy.)

Two

FOUNDERS AND BUILDERS

McClure Bottom around 1920. Notice the machine shop in the lower left. Six of the company's Shay engines can be seen on the yard above the shop. Sand was scooped from the river and dried in the small building near the engines for use on the locomotives to keep the wheels from slipping on a steep grade or wet rail. The place that later became known as McClure was selected by the Virginia General Assembly in 1880 as the governmental seat for the newly formed county. Citizens in the western part of the county were not satisfied with the chosen site and struggled to have it relocated. While the dispute was being settled, the county seat was located at Nora, about three miles south. A map of the area showed only McClure River, not McClure the town. Legend says the stream and the town were named for an explorer who was killed by Native Americans. (Photograph courtesy of Dennis Reedy.)

FRYING PAN CAMP. Camp cars are pictured on Frying Pan Creek. The cars were the solution to the problem of transportation to logging camps. The store (or commissary) and office were usually combined on the end of the string of cars. The camp stores were well stocked. On each end of the lobby were the sleeping areas—railroad cars accommodating 16 to 20 men each. (Photograph courtesy of Dennis Reedy.)

THE FOUNDER AND HEIR. Jim Damron (left) assists W. M. Ritter as the great lumber baron makes his last trip to the Red Jacket mine in September 1947. Jim Damron started with the Ritter Lumber Company as a laborer at the planing mill at McClure. Damron, a native of Clintwood, operated a taxi before going to work for Ritter. He would drive Ritter around the area when he visited the county. (Photograph courtesy of Dennis Reedy.)

WORK ON CANEY CREEK. Russell Stevens (left) and John Shortridge pose with their team. The road is called a pole road, over which the logs were dragged on Caney Creek around 1940. Usually logs were dragged over the ground. A crew of men called road swamps cut brush for the roads, while men known as road monkeys used picks and shovels to do the grade work. (Photograph courtesy of Dennis Reedy.)

TRAMMEL COMPANY STORE. Seen here is the company store and post office at Trammel, Virginia. The company built, owned, operated, and controlled the housing, hospitals, schools, local governments, and company stores, and it provided free land to build churches. The company store was the only place a worker and his family could use the company-issued scrip. (Photograph courtesy of Dennis Reedy.)

BIG BRANCH CAMP. The Big Branch camp in 1923 was located around Clintwood on the waters of the Cranes Nest and Pound Rivers and tributary streams. Some of the campsites in 1926 were at the mouth of Tarpon Branch on the headwaters of Cane Creek and Mill Creek 3,300 feet up the side of the Cumberland Mountains. Homes usually were of no more than one style of design, with a block of single dwellings and a block of duplexes. Company houses ran from single-dwelling duplexes, usually side by side, to boardinghouses for single men. Houses for the bosses were usually built of better materials. Rent was automatically deducted from employees' paychecks for the use of the company housing and electricity. (Photograph courtesy of Dennis Reedy.)

LICK CREEK CAMP CARS. Note the bunk beds with the white bed linens visible through the door in these camp cars on Lick Creek. On each end of the lobby were the sleeping areas. The railroad cars could accommodate 16 to 20 men in each car. This is where the single workers or those that boarded away from home would stay. (Photograph courtesy of Dennis Reedy.)

JIM DAMRON AROUND 1940. James W. "Jim" Damron was president of the W. M. Ritter Lumber Company. Jim Damron of Clintwood, Virginia, was the third president of the Ritter organization, with W. M. Pryor serving as chairman from 1935 to 1945. Later Damron would serve as chairman of the board while "Little William" Ritter was president. (Photograph courtesy of Dennis Reedy.)

HAMER LUMBER COMPANY. The J. P. Hamer Lumber Company was the only band mill remaining in Southwest Virginia by the end of the boom days. It was located between Norton and Appalachia. The mill operations had been sophisticated, with Ritter becoming famous for his parquet flooring. (Photograph courtesy of Dennis Reedy.)

RITTER'S MASSIVE OPERATIONS. The planing mill in Lower Elk is an example of how large the W. M. Ritter Lumber Company operations were. This facility had everything to manage the wood from start to finish, from the dry kilns to the loading shed to the engine room and ice plant. This also included the warehouse and steam-heated hardwood flooring areas. (Photograph courtesy of Dennis Reedy.)

FRYING PAN WORK CREW. These men are waiting to be hauled up the hill to their work site in 1927. Families lived in the wood camps rent free and were also provided free coal to burn in their cook stove. There was no electricity in the camps, kerosene lamps being used exclusively. No running water existed in the camps. As it was so difficult to get men and teams back and forth to the job sites, the temporary camps were created. These portable camps consisted of 8 to 12 railroad cars housing the camp store, boardinghouse, and lobby. The camp stores were well stocked for their limited size. If the customer wanted merchandise that was not available in the camp, a store order could be sent to the main store at Fremont or McClure. (Photograph courtesy of Dennis Reedy.)

TYPICAL MOUNTAIN COUPLE. Alexander and Melvina Hill were a typical mountain couple of the day. He was born in 1849 and lived until 1927. He and Melvina were married in 1873. It was virtually unheard of for couples in the area to divorce. It was common for the man to marry again if his wife died. (Photograph courtesy of Dennis Reedy.)

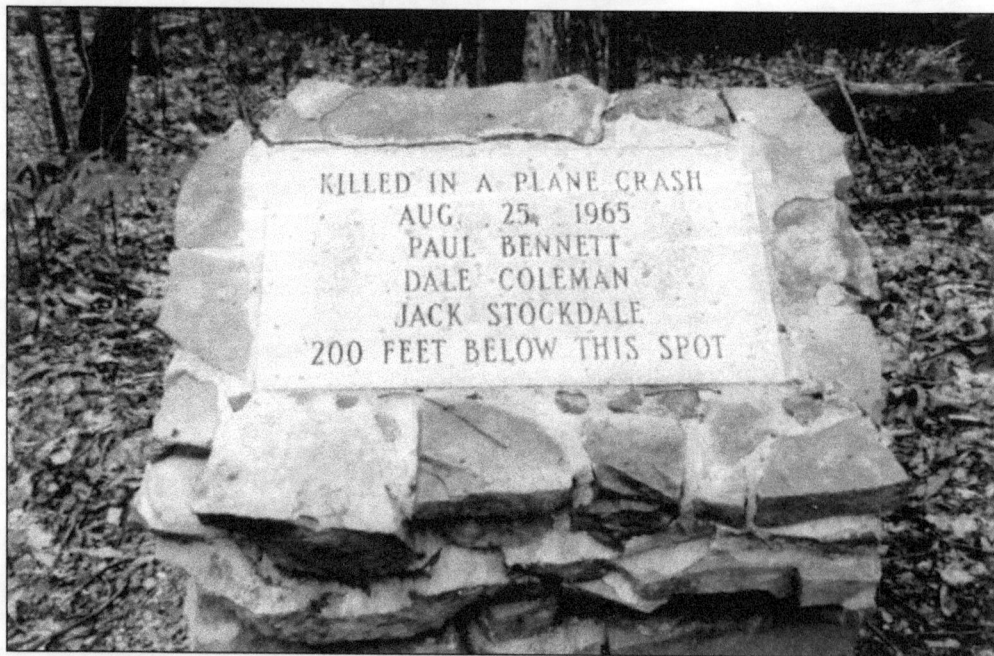

KILLED IN A PLANE CRASH
AUG. 25, 1965
PAUL BENNETT
DALE COLEMAN
JACK STOCKDALE
200 FEET BELOW THIS SPOT

PLANE CRASH MARKER. This grave marker is for Paul Bennett, Dale Coleman, and Jack Stockdale, who were killed in a plane crash on August 25, 1965. The location is known locally as Airplane Crash Rock. It is located at Birch Knob, Virginia, six miles north of Clintwood in the Jefferson National Forest. (Photograph courtesy of Dennis Reedy.)

LARGE MOUNTAIN FAMILY. The family of John Henry "Long John" and Emma (Stanley) Yates poses about 1920. It was typical for families to include 10 or more children. Usually two to three were lost in the early years to various causes of death, but it was common for parents to raise to adulthood as many as 10 to 15 children. (Photograph courtesy of Dennis Reedy.)

COUNTY JAIL LOGS. The lower story of this building contains the logs from the first Dickenson County jail in Clintwood. Justice in the mountains in the early years was very different. Many times, the citizens themselves took the matter into their own hands and dispensed justice with the Bible as the law. (Photograph courtesy of Dennis Reedy.)

POPPY JOHN AND GULF. John "Pop" Molinary stands in front of the Gulf service station. The Gulf Oil Corporation or GOC was a major oil company from the beginning of the century to the 1980s. The business that became Gulf Oil Corporation started in 1901 with the discovery of oil in Spindletop, Texas. Gulf introduced significant commercial and technical innovations into the business, including the first drive-in service station in 1911 that also offered free air to motorists and complimentary road maps. By 1941, Gulf was the eighth-largest corporation in the world and number nine in 1979. Gulf was one of the so-called Seven Sisters of oil magnets, but by the mid-1970s, the industry began to change. In 1984, the Gulf Oil Corporation ceased being an independent company when it merged with Standard Oil of California, better known as Chevron. (Photograph courtesy of Dennis Reedy.)

SANDY RIDGE TUNNEL. W. C. Hattan inspects the north portal of the Sandy Ridge Tunnel in Trammel, Virginia, around 1912. It was a long and tedious process to cut through the mountainside to build the necessary tunnels to accommodate the trains that needed to haul the coal. The tunnels opened up the area for new industry to arrive. (Photograph courtesy of Dennis Reedy.)

BOY SCOUTS OF AMERICA. Troop 42 of McClure was organized in 1951. The national Boy Scouts organization was started in 1907 by Robert Baden Powell, a lieutenant general of the British army. These scouts constructed their own boats from small wooden runners converted with canvas. Each boat cost $100 to construct. (Photograph courtesy of Dennis Reedy.)

MEAL TIME IN CAMP. These men are timber cutters at dinnertime near Lick Creek Camp, Virginia. The hours were long, but the food was plentiful. The logging companies had at least two cooks on duty at all times to prepare the meals and do the cleanup for the loggers. (Photograph courtesy of Dennis Reedy.)

THE PROPER SAW DEMONSTRATIONS. Here is W. M. Kennedy of Maben Woods demonstrating how not to carry the saw and how to carry it. (Photograph courtesy of Dennis Reedy.)

MOUNTAIN COUPLES TRANSPORTATION. These couples could be on a Sunday afternoon outing or going to visit family or friends. Transportation was primitive in the Cumberland Mountains until the logging industry started building roads to get to the timber the mountains held. Many old Native American paths were the only roads used up until that time, which meant that couples only traveled when it was absolutely necessary to take care of business such as legal matters or to pay taxes. Another major reason was for funerals or weddings. Possibly these dressed-up couples were on their way to a wedding, as they look very happy to be out on such a beautiful day with their husbands or boyfriends—probably husbands since no chaperone is evident in this photograph. Chaperones were necessary for any proper couple during their courting period before the marriage. (Photograph courtesy of Dennis Reedy.)

SOUTH SANDY RIDGE. This photograph depicts the south approach to the Sandy Ridge Tunnel showing the dump trestle and train in Dante, Virginia, in August 1914. The tunnel saved the company a great deal of money in expenses in getting the coal to market on time. That enabled them to sign contracts with larger corporations, which made the area boom for a while. (Photograph courtesy of Dennis Reedy.)

SANDY CONCRETE CAR. With the logging and mining industries bringing a boom to the county for an extended period of years, they started building. Many of the buildings that were built in the 1920s and 1930s of concrete are still standing today as a testament to the craftsmanship of those builders. (Photograph courtesy of Dennis Reedy.)

CAMP HOUSING BOOM. Sara Hatton inspects her new home at Squirrel Camp around 1912. The company housing system was quite advanced for its time. All the houses were built in a row, and there were usually one or two designs. The houses were usually painted in a distinct color such as green or white. They can still be recognized in the older parts of these communities today. The houses were usually one or two bedrooms. The renters or employees paid the company a rental fee each month for use of the house. If an employee was fired or quit, they had to pack up and leave immediately. The bosses had houses at the other end of the community. The houses were larger with a few more amenities, which were appropriate for their titles within the company. The company store, hotel, hospital, school, and church were all within that small community. (Photograph courtesy of Dennis Reedy.)

TOMS CREEK COMPANY STORE. Shown here is the large company store at Toms Creek. The company stores were vital to the community. The stores were well stocked, and delivery was free if a costumer requested it. The stores also were of service in that the loggers and later miners could buy on credit that would be deducted from their paychecks. (Photograph courtesy of Dennis Reedy.)

CLINCHCO V. CLINTWOOD. The Frying Pan and Clinchco or possibly Clintwood baseball teams take a rest. The C on the uniforms stood for both Clintwood and Clinchco. On Saturdays, the companies provided transportation to the games. The games were taken so serious that some companies recruited college players to play on their team. (Photograph courtesy of Dennis Reedy.)

44

FREELING POST OFFICE. This is all that remains of the old Freeling Post Office. The mail was originally transported from Raven, Virginia, on horseback to the area. Then the company stores started handling it. As progress arrived and the system became more sophisticated, the government started building post offices. One like this is rare to even see today. (Photograph courtesy of Dennis Reedy.)

WINTERS AT RIVERSIDE. In this picture of Riverside around 1954, the grocery store is on the right along with the Clinchco Café and Coney's service station in the distance. Winters in the mountains are notorious for shutting everything and everyone down for weeks. It is common to have snows of a foot or more. (Photograph courtesy of Dennis Reedy.)

W. M. Pryor. W. M. Pryor served as chairman and former president of the W. M. Ritter Lumber Company in 1940. The company that started with a $1,500 loan had by 1924 grown so much that its founder, W. M. Ritter, had been called to serve as an executive member of the Council of National Defense, with the start of the United States' participation in World War I. At the end of 1924, Ritter startled the nation when he gave away $3 million worth of stock to employees of his company, who deserved it by being loyal. Pres. Calvin Coolidge was so impressed that he called Ritter to the White House to discuss it and followed it with a complimentary letter in which he praised this act as a fine step towards happier employer-employee relations. This action also brought up the first test of the newly passed gift tax feature of the Revenue Act. (Photograph courtesy of Dennis Reedy.)

46

PRIMITIVE PASTOR LIPPS. The first organized church in Darwin was known as the Lost Meeting House. It was at the mouth of Honey Camp. It was the old Primitive Baptist, with Morgan Lipps as its pastor. Visiting ministers were James Smith, D. H. Riner, Billy Hale, and George Buchanan. (Photograph courtesy of Dennis Reedy.)

CHILDREN IN CAMPS. Notice the load of timber on the railroad car in the background of this photograph. The child is obviously fascinated by the camera, as photography was new in the area in the early 1920s. Children in the camps always had plenty of other children to play with, as they all lived next door to each other. (Photograph courtesy of Dennis Reedy.)

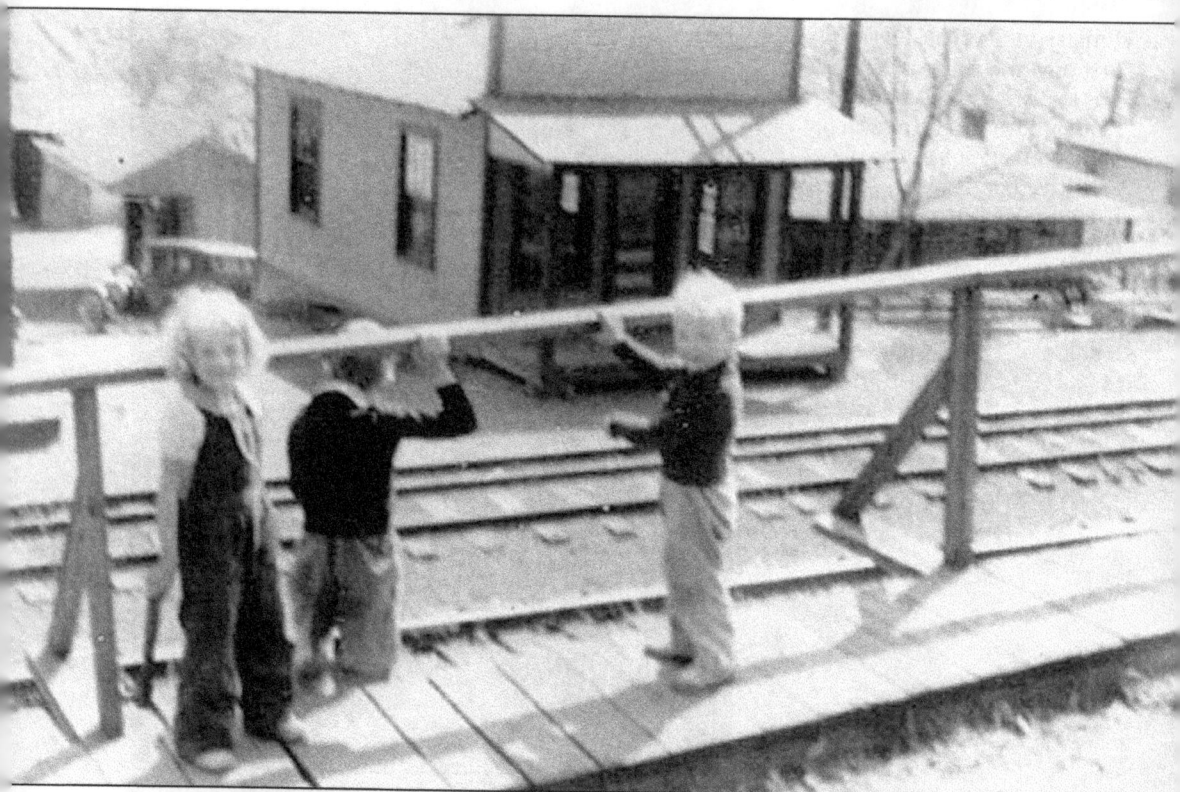

KOPP'S OFFICE AT FREMONT. The building across the tracks served as A. A. Kopp's office and later as the Fremont Post Office. These children had much to occupy them. They did not have the high-tech toys of today, but they did invent their own games such as fox and geese, kickball, and swimming in the creeks. Motion pictures were becoming popular in the 1920s, and the community buildings also doubled as movie houses. Dance clubs were formed, and the company trains carried the employees to different locations to perform and entertain the families. A hand-packed dirt tennis court was located on Caney Creek. A croquet ground was also on Caney, as was the baseball diamond. Gospel singing and basketball also helped to entertain the men and their families during their free time. The baseball games were well attended. In 1927, *Hardwood Bark* magazine stated that Lower Elk fans received a sad surprise when the "Caney Nine" defeated their invincible warriors. (Photograph courtesy of Dennis Reedy.)

Three

SCHOOLS

EARLY SCHOOL BUSES. The old Ervinton High School in Nora, Virginia, is pictured about 1936 showing two early buses. The one on the left is a Chevrolet, while the one on the right is a Ford. Both of them are about 1934 models. The men are, from left to right, Roosevelt Kiser, Buddy Stanley (the school custodian), and Everette Bise, who drove the bus for Rube Wright. Buses at that time were privately owned instead of county property. Wayne Works is widely credited with creating what became school buses. In 1886, he was making horse-drawn school carriages many people called "kid hacks" (hack is a term for certain types of horse-drawn carriages). By 1914, he had dropped a wooden kid onto an automobile chassis, and the school bus was born. But it is Dr. Frank Cyr who is the father of the yellow school bus. The color was selected so black lettering could be seen in darkness. (Photograph courtesy of Dennis Reedy.)

OLD BISE SCHOOL. The first room of this two-room building was constructed in 1915. A second room was added in 1923 by contractors Kennedy and Dotson at a cost of $2,000. This school was discontinued at the end of the 1963–1964 session. The first school was taught in an old building used for a church and Odd Fellows hall. (Photograph courtesy of Dennis Reedy.)

AN UNKNOWN OLD SCHOOL. This photograph depicts a two-room school under construction at an undetermined location within the county in the 1920s. Included in the picture are George Burchette (left), L. A. Priode, M. E. Senter, and T. Washom Bise. (Photograph courtesy of Dennis Reedy.)

THE CLINCHCO TEACHERS. These ladies of Clinchco may have been teachers. The building in the center behind them was the school at that time but was formerly the first company store built in Clinchco about 1916. A portion of the 10 seven-room apartments, one of which housed the teachers and was called the Teachers Cottage, is visible to the right. (Photograph courtesy of Dennis Reedy.)

CLINTWOOD PUBLIC SCHOOL. The Clintwood Public School and Normal College was erected in 1904. Prof. Milton W. Remines served as principal. From 1909 until 1922, the building housed the Clintwood High School and Clintwood Elementary School. The site is now occupied by the school board office. During the Civil War, the Clintwood School was used for only three months in 1865. (Photograph courtesy of Dennis Reedy.)

SUPERINTENDENT OF SCHOOLS. Willie A. Dyer served as superintendent of the county schools from 1905 until 1909. Dyer was also a schoolteacher for 13 years in the county school system. In 1901–1902, he taught at Cold Spring School and received a salary of $30 per month. The first year he taught, he received only $24 per month. In 1903, Dyer taught at Trammel. In 1904, he bought out the French Mercantile Company and sold goods at the Forks of McClure for an extended period of time. In 1905, he was appointed division superintendent of schools for the county at a salary of $20 per month. Dyer made it a point to visit all the schools within his jurisdiction. His duties included attending board meetings, issuing certificates, holding exams, and visiting schools. (Photograph courtesy of Dennis Reedy.)

BIG OAK SCHOOL. The tall gentleman behind the children is teacher Roley Stanley in 1913 with his class. Pictured are, from left to right, as follows: (first row) Virgie Owens, Eva Stanley, Bertha Owens, Virgie Stanley, unidentified, Grace Stanley, Verta Stanley, Julia Reedy, Bill Fields, Kemper Fields, Alice Fields, and ? Fields; (second row) Elise Fleming, Emma Stanley, Lula Kennedy, Willie Stanley, Leon Fields, Willard Stanley, Stewart Childress, Hattie Stanley, and Lydia Childress. It was very difficult for children to go to school in the early 20th century. The first schools were generally subscription schools. The teacher was paid a certain amount per student enrolled in the class. When farm work or chores at home demanded, the children were kept out of school to help with the work while their fathers worked in the mines or logging camps—it was a necessity to survive. Students often had to walk three or more miles to get to school in various weather conditions. (Photograph courtesy of Dennis Reedy.)

CLINCHCO TEACHERS AROUND 1941. The Clinchco teachers for the academic year 1941–1942 are, from left to right, (first row) Louise Sutherland, Glady Rudder, Dorsey Reedy, Samantha Remines, Val Hilton, Hazel C. Parker, and Janice McCoy; (second row) principal Clyde Reedy, Major Arwood, Claude Carty, and assistant principal Edgar Alley. The starting salary for teachers was $24 per month. (Photograph courtesy of Dennis Reedy.)

OLD ABNER GAP. The first Abner Gap School was a one-room building constructed of logs and mud, but later a more modern structure of planks was built. The small school fit the needs of the community when it was first settled in 1860, when wealthy landowner Samuel Endicutt and his family built in the area. (Photograph courtesy of Dennis Reedy.)

BUS RIDE AT FREMONT. Area Fremont children wait for the school bus around 1954. By 1954, children could ride a bus versus walking several miles to school like earlier generations. By the early 1950s, more parents saw the importance of sending their children to school. They willingly made the sacrifices necessary to give their children an education. (Photograph courtesy of Dennis Reedy.)

CLINTWOOD'S GREENWOOD SCHOOL. The two-room Greenwood School was built by D. G. Kelly of Clintwood in 1911 for a little over $800. In 1925, W. O. Deel was contracted to add two additional rooms at a cost of $2,800. One room was used for a cafeteria and three rooms for classrooms in later years. The school closed at the conclusion of the 1968–1969 academic year. (Photograph courtesy of Dennis Reedy.)

NORA'S LITTLE SCHOOL. The two-room Nora School was built by McCorkle Lumber Company in 1917 and used until the Ervinton School was ready for occupancy in 1936. The present-day Ervinton High School on Open Fork opened in 1955. Nora had no school until Mrs. H. F. Binns began to teach in the church. The number of pupils was irregular due to camp families moving in and out. In 1924, the lumber company moved away, so the school remained small. Nora's first name was Open Fork. Later it was called Ervinton. When the Rasnakes had the post office, they called the area Stratton. It was the county seat until Capt. John P. Chase was elected to the legislature, at which time he had the county seat moved to his home, then Holly Creek, now Clintwood. The next postmaster was Jack Dorton. Dorton named the area Nora after his wife. (Photograph courtesy of Dennis Reedy.)

THE WAKENVA SCHOOL. The Wakenva School was built in 1938 with Works Progress Administration (WPA) funds at a cost of $3,356.19. The first year of operation, Jack Hilton, who transferred from Roaring Fork, taught five months. The school had two teachers each of the next two years. The fourth year, only one teacher was at the school. The school closed at the end of the 1964–1965 academic year. (Photograph courtesy of Dennis Reedy.)

STEINMAN'S LITTLE SCHOOL. The Steinman School is seen as it looked in 1954. The school had been abandoned by this time. The name Steinman originated from the company mining coal in the neighborhood, Steinman Coal Corporation. The company began operations in 1918. The school was located on the west bank of the McClure Creek in the Willis District. (Photograph courtesy of Dennis Reedy.)

TRACE FORKS SCHOOL. The Trace Fork School was sometimes called Lyons Fork School. As there were no school buildings in the beginning, most classes were taught in old dwelling houses, churches, or stores. Trace Fork was built in 1921. It started out with only two rooms. In 1938, a third room was added. This was a joint venture with Wise County, each owning half. (Photograph courtesy of Dennis Reedy.)

BIG TOMS SCHOOL. As the Toms Creek School shows, not all county schools were simple one- or two-room structures. Coal mining started in Toms Bottom in 1917. It was located in the Breaks of the Cumberland Mountains on the CC&O Railroad line, near the Kentucky line. The Bartlick Smokeless coal mines operated close by. (Photograph courtesy of Dennis Reedy.)

STEINMAN AROUND 1950. Steinman is seen as it appeared in the 1950s. The school is the last building on the hill near the left center of this photograph. The Steinman Development Company and other companies had extensive holdings in the area. The holdings were put into the Wakenva Coal Company with C. Bascom Slemp and S. R. Jennings as officers. (Photograph courtesy of Dennis Reedy.)

THE STONEWALL SCHOOL. The Stonewall School was built in 1926 on property deeded by Nathaniel and Polly Rose to the county. Henry Ratliff served as the contractor. The Stonewall community was densely settled. The school was named after one of the citizens and ran for nine months out of the year. This was the first school to run for nine months in that area. (Photograph courtesy of Dennis Reedy.)

AN ACADEMIC GIANT. Prof. Milton Remines was a dominating figure in the academic world of Dickenson County. He served as superintendent of schools for a number of years. He had the difficult task of bringing education to a rural area that had to worry about surviving from day to day. Enthusiasm was great when Professor Remines arrived at the Hale lot near W. M. Merrick's home in 1898. He was assisted by Hattie Phipps, Alice Robinson, and James Altizer. However, around March 1902, the structure burned and the term was finished at the Methodist church. Soon a new building was erected, and the influence of Professor Remines was evident. An act was passed by the Virginia General Assembly on March 9, 1903, authorizing issuance of $3,000 to $7,000 in bonds by the Clintwood school district trustees for 25 years to complete a new building. It would be one of the most outstanding buildings in the state at that time. It was called the Clintwood Normal College. (Photograph courtesy of Dennis Reedy.)

THE OLD CANE SCHOOL. The Cane Creek School was a one-room structure built in 1913. The first Native Americans known in the county came from Russell County about the year 1850 to Cane. They captured a white girl and spent that first night on Cane Creek. The school was used for about 10 years and ran three months a year. (Photograph courtesy of Dennis Reedy.)

NEW ABNER GAP. The school was built in 1938 with the aid of the WPA at a cost of $16,000. The New Abner Gap School was unusual in that it was the only brick two-room building constructed in the county at that time. It also contained an office and conference room. (Photograph courtesy of Dennis Reedy.)

KENNEDY CONSTRUCTION COMPANY. The Middle Branch School was built in 1922 by B. F. Kennedy. It was difficult to provide supplies for the first schools. The woodpile often served for seats and one's knees for desks. The elementary spelling book was one of the few books used. Students practiced spelling aloud. (Photograph courtesy of Dennis Reedy.)

THE POOR MAN'S STORE. The exact time of the Prater settlement is unknown, but the school was built in 1935 and closed in 1969. It was sold the same year and became "The Poor Man's Store." Money was scarce, and even after a few small stores were built, the people bought the few things they needed with produce and ginseng. (Photograph courtesy of Dennis Reedy.)

THE BEAR PEN. The Bear Pen School received its name due to a bear trap. Bear Pen lies in the Cumberland Mountains. Elbert M. Fulton, later a prominent Wise County lawyer, taught there. The log building on Pound River above the mouth of Bear Pen Creek was used for religious worship as well as school purposes. Monthly meetings were conducted there for perhaps 50 years, but it later became private property and was torn down. The Bear Pen community had few settlers and in that way was similar to another former settlement, Goldsmith's deserted village. Some of the bottoms along the river have been cleared up and cultivated. While workmen were repairing the public roads, they ran across a huge cliff below the mouth of Bear Pen Creek. They found human bones embedded under the large flat rock. (Photograph courtesy of Dennis Reedy.)

WEST DANTE SCHOOL. The West Dante School was built in 1917 by B. F. Kennedy with new additions added in 1926. In the beginning, only three families lived in and around Dante. The population would grow with the emergence of mining. West Dante was first called Turkey Foot. The reason for that is the shape of the creek marker. The citizens built the school. (Photograph courtesy of Dennis Reedy.)

OLD FLINT SCHOOL. The Old Flint School is located on the lower end of Sandy Ridge. Unlike many area schools, the Old Flint School was built totally by the citizens. Citizens who could not help work on the house donated their part in money or supplies. The walls of this school are at least 10 inches thick. (Photograph courtesy of Dennis Reedy.)

BEAR PEN GRADUATES. Pictured is the graduating class of Bear Pen School for the academic year 1948–1949. The Bear Pen School was a consolidation of three schools: Brush Creek, Fairview, and Kilgore. It was established in 1918. There have been seven schools, the first six averaging five-month terms. The seventh established the nine-month school year. (Photograph courtesy of Dennis Reedy.)

OPEN FORK SCHOOL. This two-room structure was built in 1917. The date the school closed is not available, but the building was sold in October 1969, so the closing date was probably close to that. The original structure was built in 1885. The house was made of logs lapped together at each end and daubed with mud and moss, with windows two feet wide on each side. (Photograph courtesy of Dennis Reedy.)

TRACE FORK PAINTING. The old Trace Fork School is being painted around 1938. The first school was taught near Jarvey Robinson's home in an old log dwelling house by Henderson Dean. Trace Fork is sometimes referred to as Lyons Fork. The school was built in 1921. (Photograph courtesy of Dennis Reedy.)

KENNEDY AND DOTSON BUILDERS. The Viers School was built by Kennedy and Dotson in 1917 at a cost of $2,500. It was abandoned long before this photograph was taken in 1954. The first rough log schoolhouse was built on Laurel Branch in 1878. It had a fireplace about six feet wide and only two windows. (Photograph courtesy of Dennis Reedy.)

EARLY SCHOOL IN BARTLICK. The first room of this school was built in 1912. The second room was added in 1916. The school remained in operation until 1961. The first schools in Bartlick were taught in the homes that were available. The old Harve Colley house was once used as a schoolhouse. In the early 1890s, the first school was built. It was on the Harve Colley property. It was a small structure with dirt floors with a fireplace at one end. It was condemned by the school board after about five years because of its smallness. The county was in a financial crisis, and no money was available for a new school. The Turner School was used during that period of time. In 1899, Crockett Owens was paid $40 to put up the walls of a new school. Once the logs were on the site, they had a house-raising party, and a new school emerged. (Photograph courtesy of Dennis Reedy.)

THE OLD WAKENVA SCHOOL. The Old Wakenva School stands no more. Like many of the schools, churches, and buildings that started the county, the history gets lost. As generations die, they take with them the history of that area. Much of the history that exists owes that fact to superintendent of schools Joshua Hoge Taylor Sutherland when he had his teachers keep reports. (Photograph courtesy of Dennis Reedy.)

MOUNT CARMEL LEGACY. The Mount Carmel School around 1938 shows students waiting on the teacher. The school was discontinued before 1954, and little is known of its existence. The students that attended these small schools usually attended school once the farming, canning, and other household chores were completed. (Photograph courtesy of Dennis Reedy.)

THE ENDLESS STRUGGLE. The Cranes Nest School was built in 1950. The need for the school was great, as students had to be sent to the Bise, Kerr, or Dickenson Memorial High School in Clintwood. The community took a while to decide on the location because they were divided into two separate factions. Petitions went before the school board, which decided the school would be located near the Cranes Nest River by the state highway between Clintwood and Fremont. Once built, the school enjoyed a high attendance, averaging about 48 students a year. The school faced endless struggles to get equipment; at one point, only one blackboard existed for the entire school. Some of the early teachers included Mrs. Thomas M. Flannagan and Virgil Skeen. The first settler in Cranes Nest was Weddington Vanover, who built the first log house. (Photograph courtesy of Dennis Reedy.)

THE CLASS OF 1938. The Dickenson Memorial High School class of 1938 is pictured on graduation day. The ancient custom of wearing gowns and caps goes back to Europe in the 11th and 12th centuries and later at Oxford and Cambridge Universities. It was recognized that the caps and gowns gave such functions more character and were more impressive, which increased attendance at the commencement functions. (Photograph courtesy of Dennis Reedy.)

THE KENADY SCHOOL. The Walter Kenady School was built in 1913. It is one of three that are no longer existing, the others being the Pine Grove School near Lyons Post Office and Zion Hill. The patrons built the school. The seats were made of split poles. Holes were bored in the round side of the poles, and legs were driven into them. (Photograph courtesy of Dennis Reedy.)

70

THE ERVINGTON REBELS. The Ervington High School is still being used to help educate the county's young. The mascot painted on a wall is a rebel. The schools take the business of mascots seriously, putting the image on everything from class rings to the yearbook and letterman jackets. (Photograph courtesy of Southwest Virginia Historical and Preservation Society.)

DICKENSON COUNTY HIGH SCHOOL. The Dickenson County Memorial and Industrial High School serves the Clintwood area as a multi-purpose building, serving the county's academic and industrial needs at the same time. The building is used as a landmark to find one's way in the town. (Photograph courtesy of Southwest Virginia Historical and Preservation Society.)

MCCLURE'S COMMUNITY SCHOOL BUILDING AROUND 1929. The functions of community buildings in logging and mining camps were two-fold. They provided a place for a meeting, whether for the Bridge Club or for workers being instructed in the proper way to perform their jobs. A poolroom and barbershop could also be found in such buildings, as well as church and Sunday school services. The McClure community building doubled as a school. Buildings were also used for dances or socials featuring top-notch bands such as the Ohio Melody Boys, a six-piece orchestra from Ironton, Ohio, that played at the opening dance for the building on December 8, 1922. The company ran a special train from Clinchco through Fremont picking up people for the dance. There were dance clubs at both Fremont and McClure. The community building was the center of life in the mining and logging towns. (Photograph courtesy of Dennis Reedy.)

Four

CHURCHES

THE COUNTY'S LEGACY. The Bible school class poses in front of the Old Wakenva School around 1928. The school and church were the cornerstones of community life. The early revival services were held in peoples' homes. The minister stayed with the family for a few days before going on to the next town. It gave the community a chance to get outside information when it usually took weeks for news to travel from community to community and the mail took longer. People took their religious beliefs seriously, showing respect for God, family, and country. The religious groups included the Baptists and Methodists, with communities generally having at least one Catholic church. The companies that controlled the economy in the county viewed the churches in the same manner, providing the land and materials to build many of them. (Photograph courtesy of Dennis Reedy.)

ONCE A BOARDINGHOUSE. The McClure Methodist Church, pictured around 1949, was formerly a boardinghouse, or clubhouse. It was built by the W. M. Ritter Lumber Company and was called Hotel Ritter. Ritter's American log loader, in the foreground, used to cut trees and brush, was for years run by Patton Moore. (Photograph courtesy of Dennis Reedy.)

DEACONESS BINNS AND CHILDREN. Deaconess ? Binns stands with a group of children in front of the Old St. Stephens Church in Nora about 1930. The first preaching in the county was at the mouth of Hatchet. Sunday school at St. Stephens was held every Sunday with Thursday night services. A preacher would arrive every other Thursday. The deaconess handled the services otherwise. (Photograph courtesy of Dennis Reedy.)

74

BARBARA'S SUNDAY CLASS.
Barbara Parks poses with her
Sunday school class about 1953.
By the 1950s, the roads were
more accessible, making church
attendance easier for the residents.
Before that, despite bad conditions,
people would walk many miles
to attend church once a month,
visiting with family and friends
after the service. (Photograph
courtesy of Dennis Reedy.)

MISSIONARY AT RITTER. Fannie
Diffenduffer was a missionary in
Ritter's lumber camp at Stratton,
Virginia, about 1935. Ritter Lumber
provided academic and religious
opportunities and instruction for
its employees. The Frying Pan
camp was moved to Stratton
on the waters of the McClure
River in 1935. While moving
the camp from Russell Fork, to
Stratton, the store car went into
the river. (Photograph courtesy of
Dennis Reedy.)

LITTLE RACHEL CHAPEL. The little Rachel Chapel was established in 1936. Before that, it served as a school for children that had attended the Kenady School, about one and a half miles from the chapel on the main road to Coeburn. The first teacher was Belle Dotson, a local girl. Hampton Osborne from Lee County served as teacher from 1928 to 1929. The Freewill Baptist Church served as school and church. Church names and locations varied throughout the community. Sumac Grove got its name from sumacs that grew nearby, and the denomination was Primitive Baptist. The Baptists were divided into two groups: the Primitive Baptist (hardshells) and the regular Baptists (softshells). The difference between the two groups is in the belief of the meaning of the resurrection. Many members of the church would give out invitations to other members to go home with them and enjoy the food prepared as only mountain homemakers could. It was known as the "Sunday-go-to-meetin' dinner." (Photograph courtesy of Dennis Reedy.)

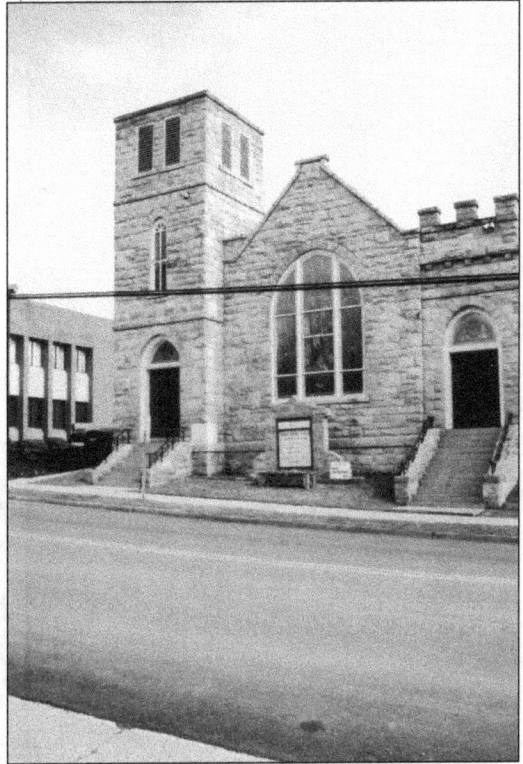

CLINTWOOD'S STAINED GLASS. The Clintwood United Methodist Church has sandstone walls and stained-glass windows. It is those windows that make the church famous throughout the community. The sandstone makes the church one of the true treasures down the street from the courthouse. The church is one of the few in the area that is built of sandstone and not wood or brick. (Photograph courtesy of Dennis Reedy.)

CLINCHCO MISSIONARY BAPTISTS. The Clinchco Missionary Baptist Church in Clinchco is one of many local churches for the county. John Smyth in 1610 founded the first Baptist church in Holland with 36 charter members. They believe that baptism is for believers only. (Photograph courtesy of Southwest Virginia Historical and Preservation Society.)

CLINTWOOD AND THE BAPTISTS. It is incorrect to apply the term church to any Baptist segment except the local church. The largest of the 20 or more Baptist groups is the Southern Baptist Convention, with over 12 million members. The largest Northern segment is the American Baptist church with 1.5 million members. When being introduced to a Baptist clergyman, is proper to call him minister. They are only addressed as pastor if they lead the congregation. The Free Will Baptist denomination can trace its origins back to 1727, when Paul Palmer organized a church at Chowan, North Carolina. The northern segment, or the Randall movement as it is commonly referred to, started with Benjamin Randall's congregation in New Hampshire. Both groups believe in the twin doctrines of free will and free salvation. In 1935, the two groups of Free Will Baptists came together under the title of the Cooperative General Association. (Photograph courtesy of the Southwest Virginia Historical and Preservation Society.)

ST. JOSEPH'S CATHOLICS. St. Joseph's in Clintwood is one of the county's few Catholic churches. St. Joseph is the husband of Mary and father of Jesus of Nazareth. He is the patron saint of workers and was declared the patron saint and protector of the Universal Catholic Church by Pope Pius IX in 1870. (Photograph courtesy of the Southwest Virginia Historical and Preservation Society.)

THE CHURCH OF CHRIST. The United Church of Christ was born out of a combination of four groups. The Congregational churches of the English Reformation with Puritan New England roots and the Christian Church of frontier days were its beginning. The other two denominations were the Evangelical Synod and the Reformed Church. They all share the commitment to religious expression. (Photograph courtesy of Southwest Virginia Historical and Preservation Society.)

THE VALLEY BAPTISTS. The Valley View Freewill Baptist Church was founded on July 14, 1914, in the Yates Gap section of the county. The early records of the church are scarce but indicate they met under an apple tree on the property adjacent to the present church. Later a church building was erected on land donated by Bishop Yates. The name Valley View was chosen by Willie Stallard. They adopted the Baptist Faith and Message, which serves as a guide to understanding their beliefs. The Baptists also have a group called the Independent Fundamental Baptists, who are independent of the Baptist convention or other associations and are more conservative in their beliefs and styles of worship. They are against rock-and-roll music and things that are deemed worldly or materialistic. (Photograph courtesy of the Southwest Virginia Historical and Preservation Society.)

Five

PEOPLE AND PLACES

UNCLE DAN TICKLE. Dan Tickle (foreground) served as woods superintendent at the Big Branch camp at the mouth of George Fork on Pound River in 1930. From left to right are (in the background) C. O. Triplett, Dee McKinney, and Dave and Ernie Tickle; (on the walkway) Audrey McKinney and Hazel Triplett holding Clark Triplett. Wood camps were accessible by the company's narrow-gauge railroads. There were gasoline motorcars for the superintendents. The people lived in a time that showed force of character, when nothing was a guarantee from day to day. The basic means of survival required strength and persistence on a daily basis, which was something these people had in abundance. They survived, built homes, raised families, paid their bills and taxes, went to church, and had an unshakable faith in God. (Photograph courtesy of Dennis Reedy.)

THE STANLEY BROTHERS. From left to right are Pee Wee Lambert, Leslie Keith, and Carter and Ralph Stanley in the early 1940s. They played the ballads that were brought from England to the southern Appalachian Mountains, where for centuries they were passed from father to son. (Photograph courtesy of Dennis Reedy.)

THE CONVICT CAMP. This photograph depicts the convict camp on site of the lumberyard at the mouth of Caney Creek in the early 1950s. The land and houses at Fremont went to the Clinchfield Coal Corporation. The towns were divided into 120 lots and sold at auction by the Johnson Land Company. The area that had been the McClure band mill became the convict camp. (Photograph courtesy of Dennis Reedy.)

SWIMMING ON CANEY CREEK. The old swimming hole near the mouth of Caney Creek is pictured in 1929. A portion of Caney yard can be seen in the background. Unlike children of today, children of the 1920s had limited forms of entertainment and had to find ways to amuse themselves. They invented games to play. (Photograph courtesy of Dennis Reedy.)

COMPANY STORE FLOODING. One of the W. M. Ritter Lumber Company stores is seen after the 1957 flood. Notice the overturned building on the left and pumps and hoses in the road. Floods and fires were a common worry for the company officials as well as the residents of camp towns. The people were used to the floods and the destruction that followed them. (Photograph courtesy of Dennis Reedy.)

LUNCHTIME ON LICK CREEK. The Lick Creek camp crew takes lunchtime in 1923. W. M. Ritter Lumber Company was known for having good cooks who always prepared plenty of food for workers. The cooks would start about 3:45 a.m. in order to have the breakfast meal prepared at 6:00 a.m. Bacon, sausage, eggs, biscuits, preserves, and coffee were served on two large tables in the dining room. Dinner and supper meals consisted of beans, potatoes, cabbage or slaw, corn bread, pork or other meats, and pies. The cook received a salary of $25 a month. Immediately after breakfast, the cook and one helper would start dinner, which was served from 11:00 to 12:00. If all went well, they might get to rest about 30 minutes or an hour while dinner was served. If a cutting crew couldn't leave the job site, then dinner was taken to them. (Photograph courtesy of Dennis Reedy.)

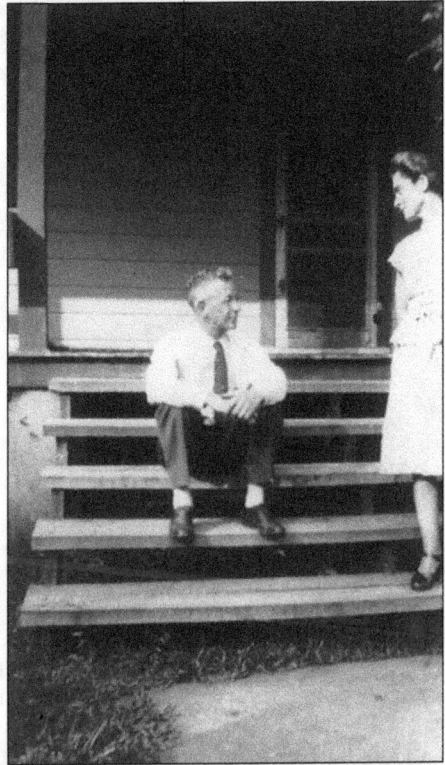

SUPERVISOR OF STORES. Giles Fink, supervisor of stores, sits on the steps of the company store conversing with Mrs. Don (Elizabeth) Weaver at Fremont around 1939. He recalled how he had started as a drag man and quickly advanced. He often related that if a moonshine still was found in operation, the cutting crew pulled back, no matter how many good logs had to be left. (Photograph courtesy of Dennis Reedy.)

THE TRAMMEL CLUBHOUSE. This picture of Trammel shows the company store, clubhouses, residences, and the boardinghouse. W. M. Ritter had a reputation for good food and clean boardinghouses for out-of-town people traveling by train to the area. The company store, clubhouse, and boardinghouses were a necessary part of camp life. (Photograph courtesy of Dennis Reedy.)

CHICKENS FOR DINNER. Hattie Hall (left) and Nita Ratliff prepare chickens for dinner. Nita Ratliff started working for Ritter in the Caney camp boardinghouse in the 1940s. She helped cook for about 100 men. She prepared three meals a day—breakfast, dinner, and supper at the camp, with carryout lunch for the men that were at cutting sites. (Photograph courtesy of Dennis Reedy.)

NOAH THE TEAMSTER. Noah Tiller, pictured around 1927, was born in the Duty, Virginia, area and received his education in the public schools. In 1908, he started working for the Honaker Lumber Company as a teamster and was later promoted to camp foreman. When the Honaker Company sold out, Noah went to work for Ritter as a skidder foreman on Lick Creek. (Photograph courtesy of Dennis Reedy.)

FREMONT AROUND 1920. As late as 1915, a topographical map of the county produced by the State of Virginia Geological Survey showed no village named McClure and only six houses in the vicinity of the town. The map did not show the McClure River, formerly known as McClure Creek. Legend says the town was named for an early explorer to the area. Fremont was the first of the Ritter Company's operations to be constructed in the county. Work began in 1916 with the clearing of laurel thicket for the sawmill, and the first lumber was produced in early 1917. In addition to the mill, the Fremont community contained about 75 residences, a combination store and office, a post office, a hotel, a community building, a school, and a railway station. It was named for John C. Fremont, a candidate for the presidency in 1856 who was employed as a surveyor on one of the small lines that became part of Clinchfield. (Photograph courtesy of Dennis Reedy.)

HURLEY IN 1928. The Hurley mill and community is pictured in 1928. Hurley was part of the third division of the four W. M. Ritter Lumber Company sawmills and considered the safest of the mills in that area, unlike the Lower Elk mill—around 1930, the roof of the planing mill fell in, injuring 11 workers, some seriously. The injured were loaded on a flat car and taken to the company hospital. (Photograph courtesy of Dennis Reedy.)

IRON MAN FULLER. Claude "Iron Man" Fuller played for No. 9 Mine in Clinchco, Virginia. He never missed a shift of work and would often work two shifts a day, thus the name "Iron Man." He signed with the New York Yankees for $168 per week and played six weeks of minor-league baseball. (Photograph courtesy of Dennis Reedy.)

McClure at Noon. The McClure Hotel is seen here along with the sheds for storing flooring and planing-mill stock. This photograph was taken just before the noon whistle had blown. There were usually about 20 to 30 boarders in the 20-room hotel to cook for. The whistle system was used as a means of telling everyone what time it was. (Photograph courtesy of Dennis Reedy.)

Willie at Work. The log Willie Ratliff sits on measures 16 feet by 35 inches and contains 882 board feet of lumber. The company preferred 80 percent of their logs to be 14 to 16 feet long. The largest log in a tree was the one cut at the stumps just above the ground. It was called the butt cut. (Photograph courtesy of Dennis Reedy.)

89

RITTER CAMP SPORTS. This early Fremont basketball team in the early 1950s is, from left to right, (first row) Fred Herndon, Lloyd Rose, Kent Chapman, Bill Breese, and Slick Carlton; (second row) Danny Hale, Bill Carlton, Bobby Dingus, Ray Reedy, Charles Breese, and Arthur Lambert. Basketball played an important role in community life in Fremont during the 1950s. Company officials took the sports very seriously. Baseball teams and basketball teams were started in the camps as entertainment. People were hired and fired based on their sports abilities. The companies provided transportation to and from the games. They brought in college players in an attempt to beat the competition. The teams were very difficult to beat, as both teams were in good physical shape considering the jobs they held. (Photograph courtesy of Dennis Reedy.)

THE RITTER FAMILIES. These are members of the various families that lived and worked for the W. M. Ritter Lumber Company at Frying Pan camp in the early 1920s. Those who are identified are (standing) Stella Triplett (second from left, in apron), Mattie Rose (third from left), Ona Breeding (fourth from left), and Charles Triplett holding son Archie (far right); (seated from left to right) Maude Rich, Alma Hinkle, Mag Taylor, Della Chambers, and Lorina Triplett. (Photograph courtesy of Dennis Reedy.)

CABIN FORK CHICKENS. Youngsters had various chores like feeding chickens at the camp on Cabin Fork of Frying Pan Creek. Families lived in the wood camps rent free. Supplies were hauled to the store and boardinghouse regularly by boxcar. Meals were prepared for 50 or more men. A bell located at the kitchen door was rung when a meal was ready. (Photograph courtesy of Dennis Reedy.)

THE FREMONT CLUBHOUSE. The clubhouse at Fremont is seen as it appeared around 1922. Hotels or boardinghouses at Fremont and McClure were more often referred to as clubhouses than hotels. There was only one clubhouse at Fremont. It fed hundreds of hungry workers for nearly 30 years. The meals were prepared by a Native American, black, or white cook. (Photograph courtesy of Dennis Reedy.)

MCCLURE'S OLD POST OFFICE. This photograph depicts the building that served as the McClure Post Office after it was moved from the company store. When this facility was constructed, the McClure Post Office was established with Giles J. Fink as postmaster on November 18, 1919. Fink, like many Ritter employees, had several jobs during the course of his career with Ritter. (Photograph courtesy of Dennis Reedy.)

AMERICAN LOG LOADER. From left to right are Lum Moore and Dick Dutton, tong hookers; Palton Moore, loader man; and Asa Bartley, top loader man, in Big Branch Woods in 1929 with the American log loader. The American log loader was made by the American Hoist and Derrick Company. The log loader had the ability to swing. The first use of this loader appears to be about 1929. In 1892, the American Manufacturing Company became the American Hoist and Derrick Company. The American log loader changed the way logs were cut. The early mills had depended on water transportation to ship logs to the mills. They would tie the logs together to form rafts to float them downstream to the sawmill. Then railroads came along and built their own rail lines, often called dummy lines, to get the logs to the mill. (Photograph courtesy of Dennis Reedy.)

DAN THE RAILROAD MAN. Dan Tickle, pictured around 1927, got his first job with the Norfolk and Western Railway Company in 1890 on the section crew as a reward for flagging a passenger train and preventing a serious wreck. In 1895, Tickle went to work for Ritter Lumber Company. He quickly advanced from yard foreman to assistant superintendent. (Photograph courtesy of Dennis Reedy.)

THE SILAS DEELS. Silas and Ethel Deel are pictured on their 51st wedding anniversary. They had 52 grandchildren and 33 great-grandchildren. Silas Deel started working at Squirrel Camp between Clinchco and Fremont. He helped put up the steel at Big Branch and later worked at McClure Woods. The track crew worked hard and generally received low wages. (Photograph courtesy of Dennis Reedy.)

BLOCK OF HEMLOCK. Noah Tiller and his saddle horse are seen on a large block of hemlock. In the early 1900s, Ritter left huge amounts of hemlock in the forest, since no market existed for it at that time. Later it became a desirable material because of lasting quality and resistance to termites. Ritter lost several million feet of this timber. (Photograph courtesy of Dennis Reedy.)

DRY LUMBER LOADING. Inspector ? Smith and a crew load dry lumber for shipping. Different species of tree such as oak, maple, poplar, beech, and others are kiln-dried on different schedules set up by the Forest Products Laboratory according to the moisture content of the wood. Moisture content is scheduled by cutting a one-inch section of the board and weighing the sample. (Photograph courtesy of Dennis Reedy.)

SWAMPY CYPRESS LOGS. Logging was difficult no matter the area it was cut in, but no area was as difficult as the river swamps. This log is from the Collecton Cypress Company. In addition to cypress, the Cypress Company also cut gum from the swampy areas in South Carolina and Georgia. Ritter wanted to see if his business could succeed in different areas and climates. He and his associates had to build several railroads to reach timber holdings and to get them to the sawmill plants. Most of the early sawmills were circular mills, operating only two to five years at a particular location from 1890 to 1905. In 1899 at Dry Fork (also known as Ritter and Avondale), band saws were introduced. This marked a new development in Ritter's type of manufacture, and therefore the mills were fewer but larger. (Photograph courtesy of Dennis Reedy.)

Six

INDUSTRY

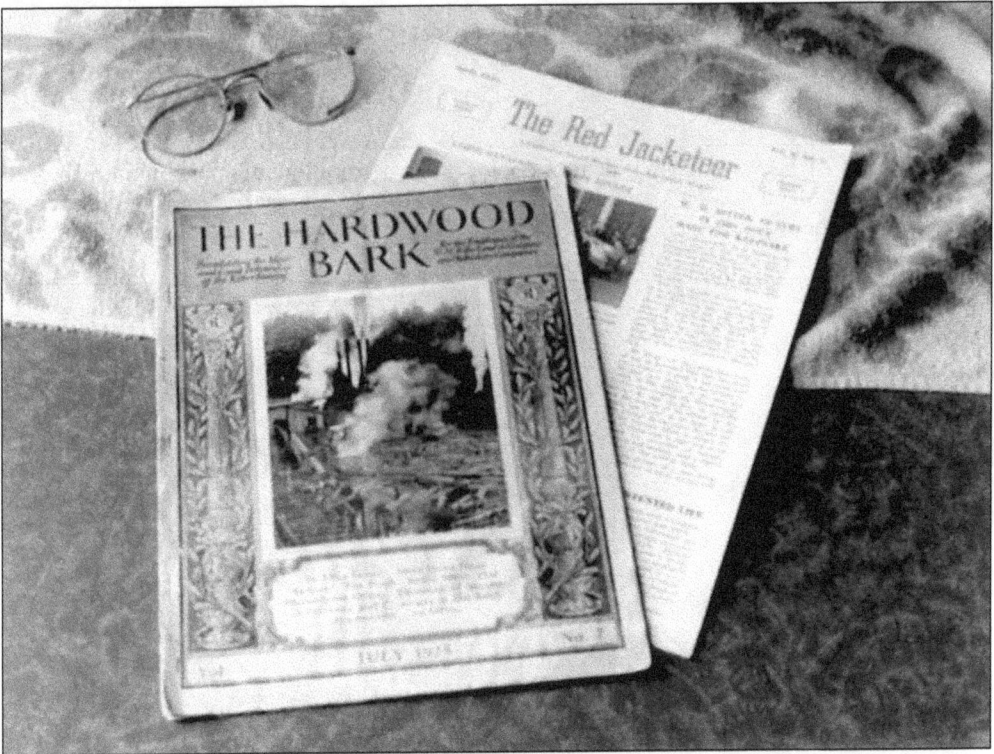

THE HARDWOOD BARK MAGAZINE. The *Hardwood Bark* and *Red Jacketeer* magazines were published by the Ritter Lumber Company and given free to its employees. These magazines contained pictures and news items from all of Ritter's operations as well as jokes and items of general interest to the lumber industry. *Hardwood Barks* contained 22 to 28 pages and measured about 7.75 by 10.5 inches. Ritter Lumber Company dominated the industry in the county and changed life in the county by opening the area up with its logging and railroad operations. Ritter provided jobs from 1890 until 1929. From 1929 until the late 1980s, Clinchfield Coal Company would be the major source of employment. The county is changing in an attempt to capitalize on the tourism industry. (Photograph courtesy of Dennis Reedy.)

POPLAR LOGS AT BANDY. A great deal of poplar and basswood was stacked high on the hill at Fremont and McClure. This enabled the lumberyards to be larger and provided better air circulation for the wood, which reduced the chances of sap staining. (Photograph courtesy of Dennis Reedy.)

MINERS AT WORK. Ritter Lumber Company mined coal to supply its own needs—for the homes, offices, and buildings of the company. The coal mine had been owned by the Clinchfield Coal Corporation and leased to Ritter. The mine was located one mile north of Fremont. It usually employed about 14 men. (Photograph courtesy of Dennis Reedy.)

AMUSEMENTS FOR THE CAMPS. Von Shores and his airplane, a Waco with air-cooled Warner-Scarch radical engine, rest at the landing field along the Powell River at Big Sandy Gap around 1930. Holders of these photographs were entitled to one free chance to win the airplane in the photograph after 1,600 of those photographs were sold. (Photograph courtesy of Dennis Reedy.)

MIDDLETOWN BLACK WORKERS. This group of railroad workers in the early 1920s lived in a group of houses between Fremont and McClure known as Middletown. When McClure was built, blacks lived at Middletown, and the area was commonly called Colored Town. The blacks were completely segregated from the white community. They were run out of town around 1930. (Photograph courtesy of Dennis Reedy.)

DRAY WAGON WORKERS. Bob Laws and Homer Barrett ride in the dray wagon at Fremont. Delivery vehicles, whether wagon or truck, were referred to as drays. A truck replaced the dray wagon at McClure around 1930. A one-horse wagon was used at Fremont until the operation closed around 1939. At Fremont, the dray met the train and hauled the mail. (Photograph courtesy of Dennis Reedy.)

SHAY NO. 949. The Shay engine No. 949 had pinion gears. A slip joint for expansion of the driveline and a universal joint for bending of the shaft can be seen to the right of the wheels just under the cab steps. The Shays used in the county weighed between 36 and 42 tons. (Photograph courtesy of Dennis Reedy.)

THE MCCLURE BRIDGE. The railroad built across McClure River in 1927 led to the Caney yard. In addition to the large bridge across the McClure River at Fremont, spans of unique construction were also built across Cranes Nest, Pound, and Russell Fork Rivers. To accommodate a large flow of water, such bridges required the use of piers instead of wooden timbers. (Photograph courtesy of Dennis Reedy.)

RITTER'S FAMOUS FLOORING. This house had Ritter parquet flooring laid in the basket-weave design. The parquet flooring came in three designs: herringbone, block, and basket weave. Some of the smaller pieces of flooring were glued together or fastened together with metal strips to form blocks. The finished product had a mirror-like shine. (Photograph courtesy of Dennis Reedy.)

RITTER FLOOR ADVERTISEMENT. This is from the September 1928 issue of *House and Garden* magazine. Ritter gained a worldwide reputation for his quarter-sawn oak parquet flooring. The flooring found its way into some of the finest homes and commercial buildings in the United States and abroad. (Photograph courtesy of Dennis Reedy.)

BIG BRANCH CAMP. The Big Branch camp is not a tourist camp but one that has the look of a trim Methodist summer resort. Notice how clean and neat the camp is. That is due to the diligence of Dan Tickle, the woods superintendent. (Photograph courtesy of Dennis Reedy.)

STEAM ENGINE BRAKEMAN. Rabbit Pittman is pictured with part of a steam engine that ran a band mill. Rabbit was a lifelong Ritter employee starting at the Fremont School. He then went to work at the logging camp above McClure at Stratton as a left-handed spike driver. He would later become a fireman and brakeman on the log train. (Photograph courtesy of Dennis Reedy.)

RITTER PAY STUB. This pay stub is for Lawson Ramsey from the Ritter Lumber Company. Wages were typically low and the hours were usually long. Until organized labor arrived, similar conditions prevailed in the mining industry as well, since mining was the only alternative to the logging jobs. Wages plummeted during the 1930s as the country's economy was crushed in the Depression. (Photograph courtesy of Dennis Reedy.)

McClure Lumber Builders. The McClure Lumber and Builders Supply occupied this Quonset building in September 1948. In 1951, the old Ritter clubhouse was purchased by the Herndons and they converted part of the building to a store. (Photograph courtesy of Dennis Reedy.)

Frying Pan Camp. The employees of the Frying Pan camp are pictured in the 1920s. The county had three large camps: Big Branch, which provided logs for the mill at Fremont; Lick Creek; and Frying Pan. Both Lick Creek and Frying Pan served the McClure mill. Smaller auxiliary camps were constructed as needed. (Photograph courtesy of Dennis Reedy.)

SHAY NO. 19. The Shay No. 19 C/N 1568 carries logs to the mill in 1958. Ritter purchased this engine, a 1905 three-truck standard-gauge of 65 tons, from Elk River Coal and Lumber Company in 1958. The engine worked at Dry Gulch and Tombstone Railroad out of Wytheville, Virginia. (Photograph courtesy of Dennis Reedy.)

PLANT NO. 32. The Plant No. 32 tipple took coal from two separate directions. The coal industry in the county was competitive throughout the world. Plant No. 32 produced more coal than any other coal producer in the area. Ritter mined coal to supply its own needs, and only later did it expand from the lumber to coal industries. (Photograph courtesy of Dennis Reedy.)

CUMBERLAND MOUNTAIN CAMP. C. O. Triplett is seen in the Big Branch camp in the Cumberland Mountains. Life in the wood camps was difficult. Many times, the locomotive engineers accommodated the camp residents by taking them to Fremont or McClure to see the moving pictures or to a ballgame. A boxcar scattered with straw or perhaps a gondola were filled with people for the ride. (Photograph courtesy of Dennis Reedy.)

RITTER CUTTING CREW. The Ritter cutting crew fell a poplar. The crews brought down the monarchs of the forest with crosscut saws and double-bitted axes. As soon as rights to timber had been gained, crews in the woods went to work. First skid roads were built into an area for the teams of horses to pull the logs over. (Photograph courtesy of Dennis Reedy.)

CROSSCUT SAWING CREW. Ezra O'Quinn (left) and Morgan Duty work. Notice the boots and leather leggings and the crosscut saw. Grease was often applied to pole roads on level grades to lessen the resistance of the logs. Timber cutters were paid by board feet in the logs they cut—$1.75 per 1,000 board feet in the early 1930s. (Photograph courtesy of Dennis Reedy.)

PAUL BUNYAN WORKS. Driver Paul Lee is seen with his team on Caney Creek in 1940. Paul was known as "Paul Bunyan." Men like him worked in steep places, where logs would skid too fast to handle. Some places were so steep, rugged, and otherwise inaccessible that horses couldn't be used. Skidders were used instead. A skidder was a steam-driven hoist engine that pulled logs. (Photograph courtesy of Dennis Reedy.)

CANEY CAMP FOREMAN. Noah Tiller, woods superintendent (left), and Luther Crabtree, camp foreman in 1935, are seen with a new team from Ohio. Long manes and tails would be trimmed by blacksmith Frank Fletcher before the horses went to work in the woods. Most horses were bought in Ohio, but some were purchased in Vermont. (Photograph courtesy of Dennis Reedy.)

MOVING 2,500 LOGS. Logs were brought across the ridge between Prater Creek and the Tilda Anderson Branch of the Russell Fork with teams, tractor, and the Lidgewood skidder by the Frying Pan crews. When this photograph was taken, Sam Counts and his crew had just completed a logging railroad to these logs. (Photograph courtesy of Dennis Reedy.)

THE AMERICAN LOG LOADER. The American log loader crew poses. Log cars did not run underneath the American log loader. Instead it swung around, picked up an empty car, and set it ahead for loading, working through the entire trip in this manner. Sometimes the log cars were set off to the side of the track if there was room. (Photograph courtesy of Dennis Reedy.)

McCLURE SAWMILL. The McClure pond is filled with logs and lumber waiting to be staked in this 1925 scene of the McClure mill during its peak of operations. The sawmill was a large two-story affair. The head saw, edger, trimmer, and other machinery used in the actual production of the lumber were located on the second floor. (Photograph courtesy of Dennis Reedy.)

THE FREMONT MILL. The Fremont mill is seen as it appeared around 1920. Ritter Lumber's dimension mills supplied a new breed of companies. One interesting customer of yellow poplar and basswood dimensions was A. I. Root Manufacturing Company of Medina, Ohio, said to be the largest producer of beekeeper supplies. A lot of the poplar dimension was used to make washboards. (Photograph courtesy of Dennis Reedy.)

COUNTS RAILROAD CREW. The Sam Counts railroad crew works on the railroad track. From left to right are Paul Selfe, Homer Harlow, Sam Counts, Dave Silcox, Will Bostic, Garland Yates, Starlin Duty, Dock Bostic, and Tom Owens. The actual laying of track was done by hand. It was back-breaking manual labor. (Photograph courtesy of Dennis Reedy.)

MITCHELL BRANCH TIPPLE. The No. 32 tipple and company houses were along Mitchell Branch. Note the wooden railway cars laden with coal. The bulk of coal operations, with a capacity of 8,000 tons per day, were located at Red Jacket on the main line of the Norfolk and Western Railroad. (Photograph courtesy of Dennis Reedy.)

FIREMAN AND BRAKEMAN. Deward Presley (left) was fireman and John Henry Nickels (right) was brakeman for engineer Bill Fletcher on the Big 1 on Caney about 1940. John Henry started working for Ritter as a tong hooker and worked over 48 years for the company. He worked at Blackey, McClure, Race Fork, New River, and Coal Mountain. (Photograph courtesy of Dennis Reedy.)

THE CARPENTER CREW AROUND 1949. From left to right are Jeno Stapleton, Leonard Stanley, Jack Fields, Ray Conley, and Rice Fields. Rice, or C. R. as he was known, helped build the houses, store, boardinghouses, mill, and lumberyards for W. M. Ritter. He also worked at the McClure planing mill when he wasn't needed elsewhere. (Photograph courtesy of Dennis Reedy.)

LITTLE ONE ENGINE. Arthur Patton pauses for a smoke in the "Little One." The engineer had the best job of any railroad worker. When operating the train, he was always seated inside out of the weather. Engineers usually started out as brakemen. The routes taken by Ritter's railroads through the county were many. In the 1930s, the line was extended. (Photograph courtesy of Dennis Reedy.)

Seven

PITTSTON V. UMWA
STRIKE

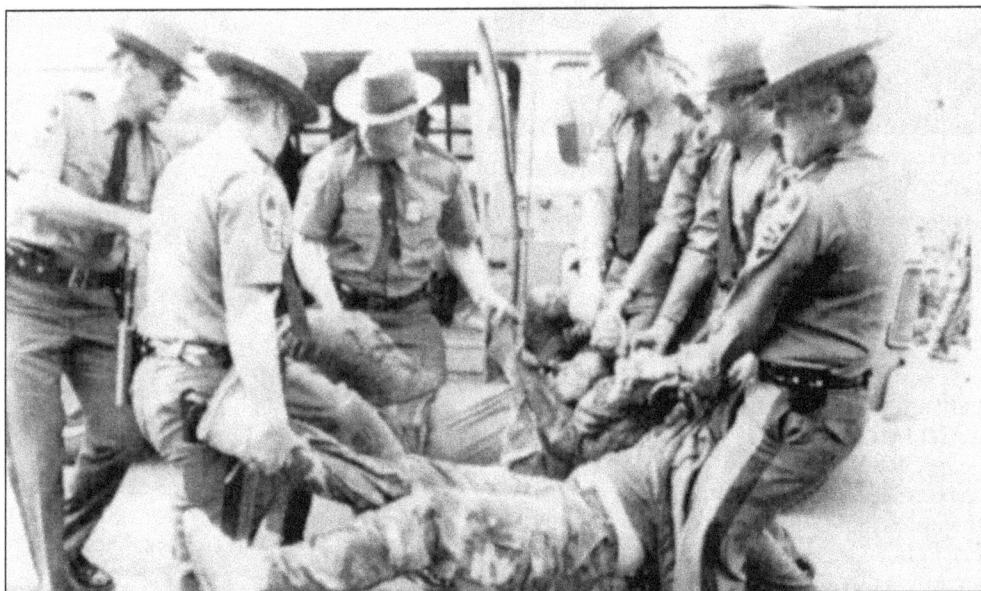

PITTSTON V. UMWA. On April 5, 1989, United Mine Workers of America (UMWA) president Richard L. Trumka announced that the miners were striking against Pittston Coal Group and its corporate parent, the Pittston Company, over allegations of unfair labor practices. The coal miners had worked 14 months without a contract at Pittston Coal Group mines. The 1,700 UMWA members in three states said they were striking for job security and medical benefits. Pittston said it needed flexibility to stay competitive in world coal markets as an exporter of coal for steel making. The company began hiring replacement workers as soon as the miners walked off their jobs. The battle that started between Pittston Group and the miners would result in U.S. marshals and state police struggling to maintain order. Judges on the state and federal level would be the ultimate authority in settling the strike after millions of dollars in fines had been imposed against the union. (Photograph courtesy of the *Dickenson Star.*)

Gov. Gerald Baliles. Gov. Gerald Baliles was governor of Virginia during the Pittston v. UMWA strike. The governors of Virginia, Kentucky, and West Virginia had agreed not to intervene in the strike. The governors had asked for a 30- to 60-day cooling-off period. The union delayed the strike until April 5, 1989, based on that request. (Photograph courtesy of the *Dickenson Star.*)

Federal Judge Becomes a Mediator. Federal judge Glen Williams was responsible for bringing the union and Pittston Coal Group together in an attempt to resume bargaining talks. Judge Williams called both sides to the meeting in an effort to restore some normalcy. Judge Williams became concerned when union members defied his court order to stop civil disobedience. (Photograph courtesy of the *Dickenson Star.*)

Judge Donald McGlothlin Jr.
Russell County Circuit Court judge
Donald McGlothlin Jr. handed down
large fines against the UMWA. The
fines would eventually reach over $64
million. Much of that would be reduced.
But his father, Donald Sr., would lose
his 4th District House seat to Jackie
Stump, one of the UMWA officials,
as a result of the strike. (Photograph
courtesy of the *Dickenson Star.*)

UMWA President Trumka.
Richard L. Trumka, the
UMWA president, called for the
strike against Pittston on April
5, 1989. The strike was a result
of a 14-month conflict that
had dominated the news in the
coalfields of Southwest Virginia.
Both sides had pushed their
agenda to the public, circulating
advertisements and booklets
on their respective positions.
(Photograph courtesy of the
Dickenson Star.)

United We Stand. The scene of Virginia state police and striking miners became common during the many months of the strike. The state police were called in to handle the "dirty work" of the strike. They had a difficult job of maintaining order during a strike that would include riots, bombs placed at a Pittston warehouse, shots fired at trucks, and general unrest. (Photograph courtesy of the *Dickenson Star*.)

Committed to a Cause. The scene of coal miners being handcuffed became common during 1989–1990. Three weeks into the strike, over 200 miners had been arrested. They were taken to the Dickenson County jail, where those giving fictitious names of John Doe were jailed and those giving their actual names were released. (Photograph courtesy of the *Dickenson Star*.)

ARRESTS ARE MADE. Mass arrests were made of striking union miners for blocking entrances to Pittston Coal Group operations. The Virginia State Police reported that arrests included Jackie Stump, District 28 president; members of the Daughters of Mother Jones, an organization of miners' and pensioners' wives, were arrested at Moss No. 3 preparation plant. (Photograph courtesy of the *Dickenson Star*.)

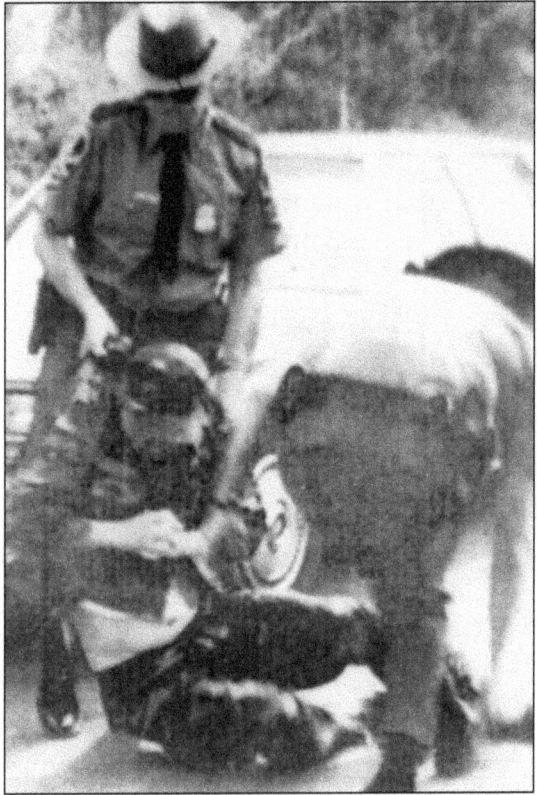

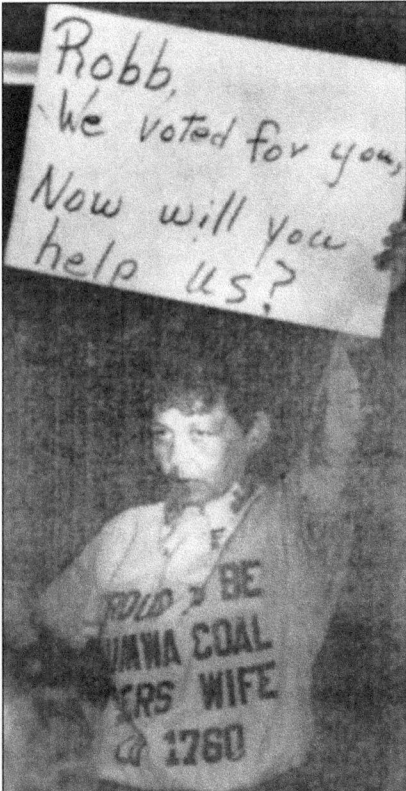

DEMAND FOR SUPPORT. As the strike stretched into months, the people demanded support from Congressman Rick Boucher, Sen. Charles S. Robb, and Governor Baliles. Governor Baliles kept his cool during the strike and urged both sides to resume negotiations and call in federal mediators. He made it clear that violence, whether instigated by management or labor, would not be tolerated. (Photograph courtesy of the *Dickenson Star*.)

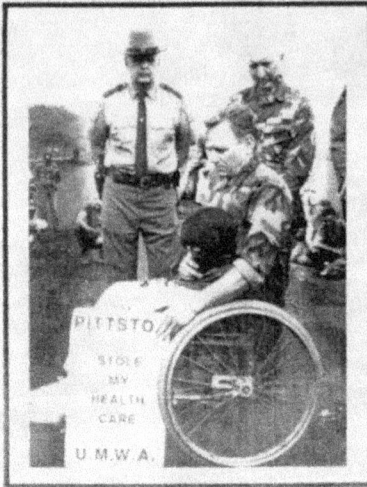

Labor In America
"We Won't Go Back"

PITTSTON
STOLE
MY
HEALTH
CARE
U.M.W.A.

UMWA/Pittston
Strike 1989-90

HEALTH CARE QUESTIONED. The UMWA stated they had received word that Pittston Company had canceled health insurance for sick, injured, and laid-off miners, while company officials claimed only laid-off and active miners lost health-care benefits. Mike Odom, president of Pittston, stated the company continued coverage for the sick and injured miners but did terminate coverage for laid-off personnel. Striking miners were denied coverage. (Photograph courtesy of the *Dickenson Star*.)

SHOTS FIRED AT TRUCK. Tension eased over the Memorial Day holiday in 1989 only to escalate a few days later, when the state police reported that shots had been fired into an occupied coal truck near one of Pittston's operations. Two small-caliber shots were fired into the windshield of the truck near Pittston's Yowling Branch mine. (Photograph courtesy of the *Dickenson Star*.)

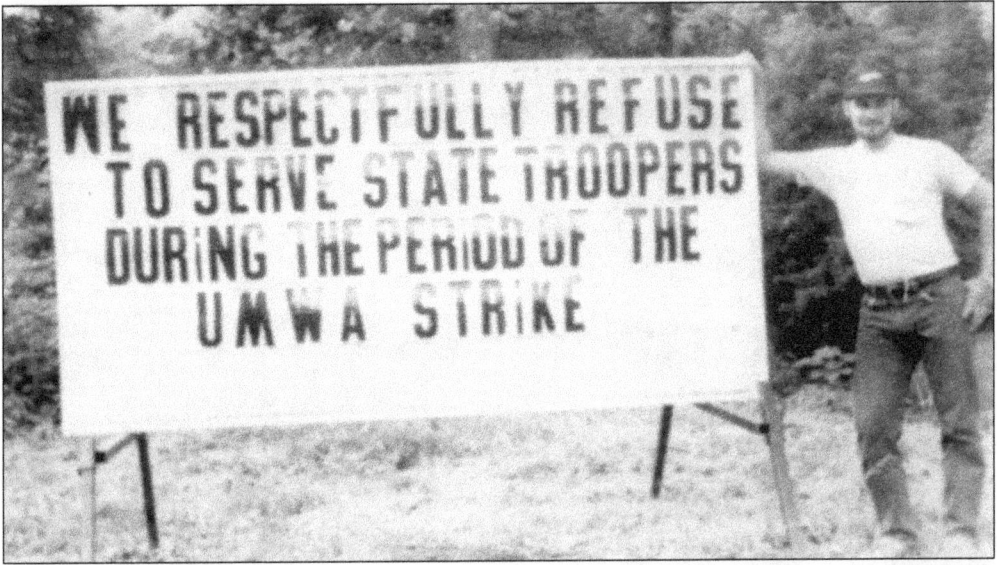

REFUSAL TO SERVE. Tempers and emotions ran high in the coalfields, with the merchants refusing to serve the state police, despite the state police's presence in the area as a peacekeeping force. The locals viewed them as hired guns for Pittston and therefore the enemy of the union. The merchants' anger rose when Sister Bernadette Kenny was arrested for allegedly impeding traffic. (Photograph courtesy of the *Dickenson Star*.)

DOUG WILDER VISITS. In a bid to become the first elected black governor in history, Lt. Gov. Doug Wilder challenged his opponent, Marshall Coleman, to visit the coalfields to witness first-hand the effects of the strike on Southwest Virginia. Wilder met with area leaders and UMWA members. (Photograph courtesy of the *Dickenson Star*.)

MINERS ON STRIKE. Striking miners from Kentucky, West Virginia, Indiana, Illinois, Pennsylvania, and Ohio flood the county's back roads in an effort to slow Pittston's coal transportation. Coal group president Mike Odom said in an interview that the influx of people had caused his company to shut down operations for much of that time. (Photograph courtesy of the Dickenson Star.)

STRIKE IS SETTLED. On February 20, 1990, the bitter 14-month-old labor strike ended. UMWA leaders made it official that 63 percent of the workers had ratified a contract settlement between Pittston and the union. "We are thrilled. It's a joyous day for everyone involved," U.S. secretary of labor Elizabeth Dole said. (Photograph courtesy of the *Dickenson Star.*)

Eight

PRESENT DAY

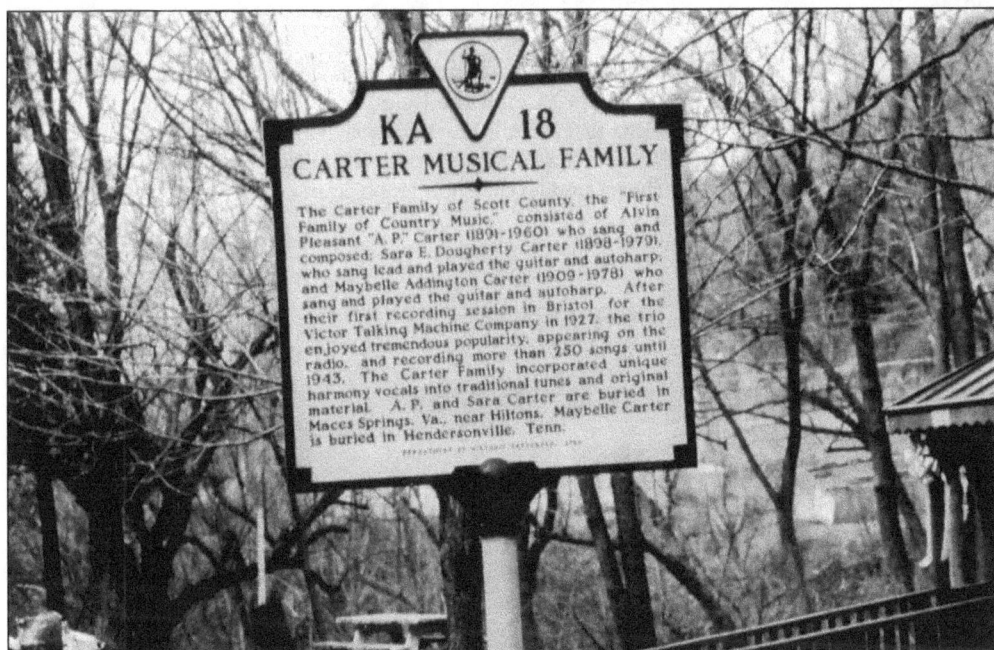

CARTER MUSICAL MARKER. Since 84 percent of Dickenson County's area is woodland, mining and lumber are still the primary employers, and farming is still performed on a small scale. What one identifies with the county is its musical legends. As the marker shows, the Carter Family was prominent throughout Scott, Dickenson, and Wise Counties. They are commonly called the "First Family of Country Music." The members included A. P., Sara, and Maybelle Carter. Their first recording session took place in Bristol for the Victor Talking Machine Company in 1927. The major industry besides farming and mining is tourism. The Breaks Interstate Park and the John Flannagan Dam provide unlimited possibilities for the outdoor enthusiast. The Ralph Stanley Museum and yearly festival provide music lovers with an insight into Ralph Stanley's beginnings in the mountains of Dickenson County. (Photograph courtesy of the Southwest Virginia Historical and Preservation Society.)

RALPH STANLEY MUSEUM. The house that is now the Ralph Stanley Museum was built by Sen. Roland Chase around 1903. It was the first brick house in Clintwood. Roland's father, Capt. John P. Chase, a founder of Clintwood, gave the adjoining land for the Dickenson County courthouse. The senator's law practice was on the ground level. (Photograph courtesy of the Southwest Virginia Historical and Preservation Society.)

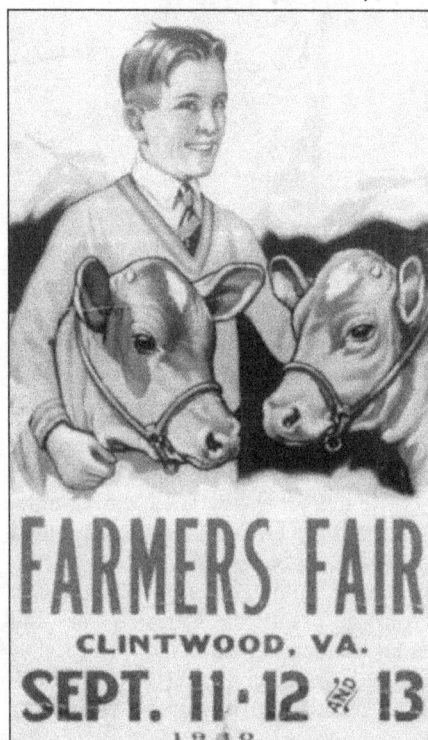

DICKENSON COUNTY FAIR. The Dickenson County Fair was a yearly event and widely anticipated, as agriculture in the county consists of small-scale, part-time farms with 10,000 acres in use. Some tobacco crops and forage are produced near the rivers. There are also 800 head of horses, primarily used for entertainment and horse shows. (Photograph courtesy of Dennis Reedy.)

JOHN FLANNAGAN DAM. The John Flannagan Dam is quite large and is part of the Big Sandy River flood protection system. The dam is named after Congressman John W. Flannagan, commonly known as the "Clintwood Cyclone." Flannagan served the Ninth Congressional District from 1931 until 1949, when he retired. The dam was completed in 1964. (Photograph courtesy of the Southwest Virginia Historical and Preservation Society.)

THE BREAKS PARK. The Breaks Interstate Park is commonly referred to as the "Grand Canyon of the South." Yearly thousands seek the beauty of the cliffs and trails. Many enjoy the amazing bird watching and rafting that is available at the park. The conference center and amphitheater make it possible for conferences to be held in the beautiful environment. (Photograph courtesy of the Southwest Virginia Historical and Preservation Society.)

CLINCHFIELD COAL COMPANY. Shown is one of the Clinchfield Coal Company warehouses located in the county. Clinchfield Coal built much of the area when it was at its peak during the mining boom. They still have some business interests in the area. However, tourism is now the main source of additional revenue and is becoming the major employer among the developing industries. (Photograph courtesy of the Southwest Virginia Historical and Preservation Society.)

THE LAST SPIKE. Trammel, Virginia, is where George L. Carter drove the last spike on behalf of the CC&O Railroad. This reenactment took place in 1990. The CC&O started in 1913. Passenger service was available shortly after. With the railroad available, the coal industry could thrive, and since then, coal has served as the major employer. (Photograph courtesy of Dennis Reedy.)

BIRCH KNOB TOWER AND OBSERVATION POINT. With an elevation of 4,162 feet, the tower is one of the area's most sought-after tourism sights. Most people at some point during hiking and sightseeing make it to see the tower high on Birch Knob in Dickenson County. (Photograph courtesy of Dennis Reedy.)

JETTIE BAKER CENTER. The Jettie Baker Center—formerly known as the Mullins Theater—was built in the 1940s. It was donated to the town of Clintwood by Mrs. Jettie Baker. The property has been completely renovated and hosts a number of talented performers. It will seat 350 comfortably. (Photograph courtesy of the Southwest Virginia Historical and Preservation Society.)

BIBLIOGRAPHY

Reedy, Dennis. *The W. M. Ritter Lumber Company—Family History Book.* Clinchco, VA: Dennis E. Reedy, 1983.

Reedy, Dennis and Diana. *Haysi, Virginia, Community and Family History.* Clinchco, VA: Dennis and Diana Reedy, 1998.

Reedy, Dennis, ed. *Schools and Community History of Dickenson County, Virginia.* Johnson City, TN: The Overmountain Press, 1992.

Goforth, James. *Building the Clinchfield.* Erwin, TN: Gem Publishers, 1989.

"Labor In America—We Won't Go Back." *The Dickenson Star.* Clinchco, Virginia: 1990.

INDEX

DISCOVER THOUSANDS OF LOCAL HISTORY BOOKS FEATURING MILLIONS OF VINTAGE IMAGES

Arcadia Publishing, the leading local history publisher in the United States, is committed to making history accessible and meaningful through publishing books that celebrate and preserve the heritage of America's people and places.

Find more books like this at
www.arcadiapublishing.com

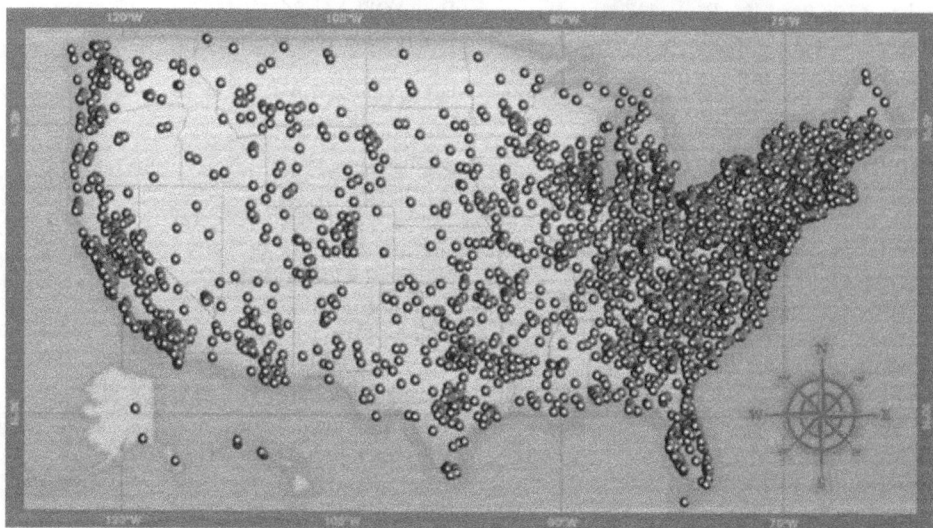

Search for your hometown history, your old stomping grounds, and even your favorite sports team.